What Is New Testament Theology?

The Rise of Criticism and the Problem of a
Theology of the New Testament

by
Hendrikus Boers

Fortress Press
Philadelphia

Aan Ida
vir soveel jare
van troue bystand

Library of Congress Cataloging in Publication Data

Boers, Hendrikus.
   What is New Testament theology?

   (Guides to Biblical scholarship: New Testament series)
   Bibliography: p.
   1. Bible. N.T.—Theology. 2. Bible. N.T.—Criticism, interpretation, etc.—History. I. Title.
BS2397.B58   230   79-7372
ISBN 0-8006-0466-0

7692E79 Printed in the United States of America 1-466

Editor's Foreword

The earlier volumes in this series have all dealt with *methods* for interpreting the New Testament and/or with certain *formal* aspects of New Testament books or shorter texts. The present volume, with its concern for New Testament theology, might appear to be a departure from that earlier program; however, it is not, for two reasons, really a departure, or at most it represents a difference of degree, not of kind. The first reason why it is not different in kind from the other volumes is that even methodological and formal considerations are not—or should not be—divorced entirely from questions of meaning. The second reason is that this book is formal in its reflections about New Testament theology. Its intention is not so much to state the content of New Testament theology as to deal, in historical perspective, with other related questions which have been and should be raised before, or along with, the effort to explicate the content of New Testament theology. How is New Testament (or biblical) theology to be defined? Where is its content to be found and how is it identified? What are its relationships to other theological disciplines—historical and systematic or constructive? For what motives has New Testament theology been pursued and what claims have been made for its truth or status? For example, it is not Professor Boers's intention to develop the meaning of Paul's understanding of justification by faith, but he does inquire into the status and significance of that motif in the work of certain New Testament theologians.

DAN O. VIA, JR.
University of Virginia

Contents

Preface

There is a certain validity in calling New Testament theology the
science of minutiae and of irrelevant nuances.

William Wrede

"Theology" is at the same time the most pervasive feature of New
Testament interpretation, and the most elusive. "Theology" is the
fundamental reason for most New Testament research, and the hidden presupposition which determines it. As a young colleague,
Richard Spencer, pointed out, the very same conception of New
Testament theology which Werner Kümmel subsequently brought
to full expression in his *Theology of the New Testament* was already
present as the principle which determined the collection of the
material for his monumental, indispensable history of New Testament interpretation, *The New Testament: The History of the Investigation of Its Problems.* Kümmel presents that history as if
everything was guided by a drive toward a growing consistency of
historical interpretation. His own *Theology of the New Testament* is
the interpretive outcome of that development. What is true on a large
scale in the case of Kümmel is similarly true of every other interpretation of the New Testament, including those which claim to be
motivated by purely academic interests.

The present volume traces the history of New Testament theology
from its beginnings in the Reformation to recent times as a means of
uncovering some of the most important factors that determine current stated and implied conceptions of New Testament theology. It is
not a discussion of fine points but an attempt to discover the basic
development as it came to expression in a number of decisive contributions by Gabler, Baur, Deissmann, Wrede, Bousset, Schlatter,
Bultmann, and Braun. The attempt is not to be accurate about details
but to uncover the basic thrust of the thought of these writers. To use

7

an expression of Bultmann, I did not try to present what they said but what they meant. In order to do so, after having read and reread the relevant contributions a number of times, underlining and reunderlining, I made a detailed list of the most significant points. These I pondered until I thought I had an idea of their authors' intentions, of the questions to which they tried to provide answers. From the perspective of each contribution I then tried to understand what was perceived as the basic issue in connection with a theology of the New Testament.

The reader will find few footnotes because I did not intend to prove points. My intention was also not to draw attention to this or that detail of an author's work but to the work as a whole. Nevertheless, when the reader picks up one of these works she or he will enjoy discovering those places I could almost have quoted. But then sometimes I did allow myself to formulate an author's thoughts from the perspective of subsequent developments to which he had not yet had access. One should give an author credit not only for what she or he actually wrote but also for what was implied in her or his work.

References in the text to works discussed are generally by translation of the titles into English. Wherever translations occur, they were made from the originals.

I would like to express a very special word of thanks to my colleague and friend, Manfred Hoffmann, who labored through the entire manuscript, cutting out excess fat and quite frequently reformulating to bring out meanings better than I myself had been able to do. I wish also to express my sincere appreciation to Theodore Jennings for his very helpful suggestions, and to Dan Via who, as a sensitive editor, made suggestions also relating to the subject matter. Although he emphasized that they were only suggestions, they proved in most cases so perceptive that they became part of the text in the final revision. A word of thanks also to Richard Hays for bibliographic assistance, and to Gregor Sebba, Max Miller, and Gene Tucker for hints that played a very important part, especially in the early phases of trying to produce a generally understandable writing such as this. To Dean Jim L. Waits, sincere appreciation for the summer grant which provided me with the free time for writing. Students in the seminar and the course I taught on the topic of this guide, apart from providing the necessary framework which makes this type of research meaningful, made many a critical comment which had its effect on this writing. To them too my sincere appreciation. Finally, I thank most sincerely Joyce Ann Baird, not only for typing the manuscript but also, through her efficiency as a secretary, for taking care of so many things.

I

The Principles Underlying a Theology of the New Testament

A. THE SUBJECT MATTER OF A THEOLOGY OF THE NEW TESTAMENT

1. A Theology of the New Testament Not as Obvious as It Might Seem

The topic "Theology of the New Testament" seems to be a very obvious one. Are not almost two thousand years of Christian theology rooted in the New Testament? If that is the case, would it not make all the sense in the world to expect that there would also be a separate discipline which focuses specifically on the theology of the New Testament itself? And yet the concept of such a separate discipline did not receive attention until around the beginning of the seventeenth century. That the church did not consider the topic of a theology of the New Testament separately for so many centuries may have been a long-standing shortcoming which was remedied only when it was given specific attention in the early 1800s.

However, when one looks into the New Testament itself, what does one find? Three rather similar *narrative accounts* about Jesus, culminating with his crucifixion and resurrection (the Gospels of Matthew, Mark, Luke); a fourth *narrative account* which reveals many similarities to the first three, but with Jesus making extended *revelation speeches* about his mission from the Father into the world (the Gospel of John); furthermore, a *narrative* of the early church in Jerusalem and the missionary journeys of Paul (the Acts of the Apostles); a number of *letters* written by Paul and other apostles, or purported to have been written by them, all with fundamentally *pastoral concerns* (the Epistles); and finally an almost bizarre *account* of the final, catastrophic events of history (Revelation). Narrative accounts, revelation speeches, letters of pastoral concern, and

9

an apocalyptic account, but nothing that could in any real sense be called a theology. Perhaps a theology is there, but certainly not obviously so. It does not lie at the surface, and maybe it did need very many centuries of reflection before the church could discover its presence in the New Testament.

2. A Theology in the New Testament?— Or Derived from It?

But what did the church find? Not a single theology of the New Testament, but a number of theologies, and in more than one way. In the first place, New Testament theology, along with Old Testament theology and, more comprehensively, biblical theology, could simply mean a theology based on or rooted in the New Testament, in contrast with dogmatic theology, that is, a theology rooted in the established dogmas of the church, whether Catholic or Protestant. This is the sense in which the designation was frequently understood in the early post-Reformation period. A theology of the New Testament in this sense is, of course, not contradicted by the apparent absence of theology in the New Testament itself, because it does not claim to be a theology which is *contained* (implicitly or explicitly) *in* the New Testament, but which is *based on* the New Testament; or at least so it would seem to be. The subsequent development contradicts this. Theology of the New Testament came to be understood fundamentally as a theology contained in the New Testament rather than being merely based on it. Maybe it was sensed that for a theology to be genuinely *based on* the New Testament, it would have to be at least *rooted in* the New Testament, which means it should inhere in the New Testament, not necessarily at the surface level but at least in such a way that it could be brought to the surface.

We are not trying here to determine what a theology of the New Testament should be but to understand how it was understood in the course of its development and how it is understood today. That would enable us to comprehend better and to evaluate the many volumes on the market which claim to present the theology of the New Testament.

3. A Single Theology or More than One; and Where in the New Testament Is It to Be Found?

In addition to the question whether a theology of the New Testament is based on the New Testament or is contained in it, there is another problem. Even when it is assumed that a theology is contained in the New Testament, there is no agreement on where in the

New Testament such a theology is found or whether it contains a single theology or more than one. In order to make this clear it is necessary to take a brief look at the way in which a few examples of such a *Theology of the New Testament* are structured. So, for example, in Rudolf Bultmann's *Theology of the New Testament* only the two central parts are called theologies, that is, "The Theology of Paul" and "The Theology of John." The two parts are preceded by a similarly extensive first part on the "Presuppositions and Motifs of New Testament Theology" and followed by a concluding part on "The Development toward the Ancient Church." The latter part is obviously not a theology, and if one has any questions about the first part, Bultmann himself states in the very first sentence: "*The message of Jesus* is a presupposition for the theology of the New Testament rather than a part of that theology itself."[1] In the original German, which has only three parts, the first and last are set off even more clearly against a single, central part on "The Theology of Paul and of John." Note, however, that this does not represent a single theology but two, that is, of Paul and of John. Bultmann's *Theology of the New Testament*, thus, is represented not by a single theology but by two, which stand in a relationship of development to each other. In addition it contains a substantial amount of other material which he himself does not consider as really part of the theology of the New Testament. The actual theology of the New Testament is to be found only in the central part(s) of his book, sandwiched in between the beginning and concluding parts.

By way of contrast, Werner Georg Kümmel does present a single theology of the New Testament "according to its main witnesses." These include not only Paul and John but also Jesus, who according to Bultmann belongs to the presuppositions of a theology of the New Testament. Still, even Kümmel's chapters distinguish between "The *Proclamation* of Jesus according to the First Three Gospels," "The *Faith* of the Primitive Church," "The *Theology* of Paul," and "The *Message about Christ* of the Fourth Gospel and the Johannine Letters."[2] The term *theology* thus appears to be in some sense more appropriate for Paul than for the others. Kümmel does also refer to the theology of John but not of Jesus. Furthermore, it does not contribute to greater clarity when he maintains that the actual presentation of the theology of the New Testament can only be the *result* of an investigation of the various forms of New Testament

---

1. Rudolf Bultmann, *Die Theologie des Neuen Testaments* (Tübingen: Verlag J. C. B. Mohr [Paul Siebeck], 1948–53), p. 1; English translation, *The Theology of the New Testament*, trans. Kendrick Grobel, 2 vols. (New York: Charles Scribner's Sons, 1951–55), 1:3.
2. My emphasis.

proclamation.[3] This suggests that the theology of the New Testament, although in the New Testament, is not to be found at the surface level of its witnesses but has to be discerned as an underlying unity by the interpreter through a consideration of the main witnesses. According to the title of the chapter on Paul, what it contains is the theology of Paul, but according to the statement above, it is not yet really theology, or at least not in the same sense as in the phrase "theology of the New Testament." The meaning of the term *theology* is not unequivocal.

Joseph Bonsirven on the other hand does not even accord John a separate treatment but includes him, along with the first three Gospels, in the discussion of Jesus. He has only one other main part, on "Saint Paul," and two lesser parts, on "Primitive Christianity" and on "Christian Maturity." In his case the ambiguity in the use of the term *theology* is most clearly evident when in the latter part he distinguishes the following three chapters: "Theology," "Christian Life," and "Eschatology." In the chapter on "Theology," he discusses "Christology," "Soteriology," "Trinitarian Theology," and "Apologetics and Christian Preaching," thus, theological subjects more narrowly defined. Within his *Theology of the New Testament,* thus, there is a subsection which is distinguishable from others as theology. As in the case of Kümmel, his usage of the term *theology* is not unequivocal.

These differences between Bultmann, Kümmel, and Bonsirven are not isolated occurrences but typical of theologies of the New Testament. Even more radical differences can be cited. They reflect fundamental disagreements among New Testament scholars on what constitutes a theology of the New Testament, formally as well as materially. Such disagreements do not necessarily reflect on the value of the theologies concerned, but they do indicate very clearly that what is meant by a theology of the New Testament cannot be taken for granted and also that it is necessary to have clarity on what "theology of the New Testament" refers to as used by any of these scholars before their work can be appreciated properly. Clearly, what they uncover as theology in the New Testament is heavily predetermined by the preconceptions they have of their subject matter.

4. The Meaning of the Term "Theology"

The fundamental problem may be, at least in part, that very fre-

---

3. Werner Kümmel, *Die Theologie des Neuen Testaments* (Göttingen: Vandenhoeck & Ruprecht, 1976), p. 18; English translation, *The Theology of the New Testament,* trans. J. E. Steely (Nashville: Abingdon Press, 1973), p. 18.

quently these scholars do not use the term *theology* in an unequivocal sense, as the above discussion, particularly of Kümmel and Bonsirven, has shown. They use the term in a more comprehensive sense with reference to the theology of the New Testament as a whole, but then distinctively within their respective works in reference to more specific matters. That Bonsirven uses the term in a more precise sense in the latter case is indicated by the more definitely theological topics—Christology, soteriology, and so on—which he discusses in the chapter "Theology" in the part on "Christian Maturities." Kümmel's usage, however, remains vague, as is clearly evident when he uses *theology* and *message* as equivalents in his chapter on John and in his "Conclusion" with reference to what his three witnesses bring to expression in common. The caution of Gerhard Ebeling is appropriate: "It is questionable to use the term *theology* so generally that every pronouncement concerning God, that each and every religious expression is considered as theology."[4]

The vagueness of the term *theology* in contemporary usage is similar to the usage of the term *philosophy*, which ranges from a precise definition, such as that of Alfred North Whitehead, to the common claim of having a philosophy which amounts to no more than certain convictions about life. Whitehead defines speculative philosophy as "the endeavor to frame a coherent, logical, necessary system of general ideas in terms of which every element of our experience can be interpreted."[5] Similarly, theology is used sometimes in the more precise sense of a coherent system of thought concerning matters relating to God, but it also ranges to a vague sense of having certain convictions concerning the same matters.

On the basis of Whitehead's definition of speculative philosophy, I propose the following as a *working* definition of theology: "A coherent, logical, necessary system of general ideas in terms of which every element of our experience concerning matters relating to God can be interpreted." The adjective *theological* will be used in a more general sense to include every statement concerning God or every religious expression insofar as it may constitute the material out of which a theology in the above more precise sense could be developed by "coherent, logical, necessary" reasoning.

The above definition is very narrow. It is not intended as a crite-

4. Gerhard Ebeling, *Wort und Glaube*, 2 vols. (Tübingen: J. C. B. Mohr [Paul Siebeck], 1960), 1:85; English translation, *Word and Faith*, trans. J. W. Leitch (Philadelphia: Fortress Press, 1960), p. 93.
5. Alfred North Whitehead, *Process and Reality: An Essay in Cosmology* (New York: Macmillan Co., 1929); now a Harper Torchbook, The Academy Library TB 1033Q (New York: Harper & Row, 1960), p. 4.

rion by means of which to determine what is and what is not theology. Nor do I suggest that the term *theology* should be used only in the very narrow sense of this definition. It will only be used as a fixed point from which to clarify and compare the ways in which theology was used by various authors mentioned below. So, for example, Scholasticism understood theology in a sense very close to that of the definition, whereas Luther's understanding was contrary to it. For Luther theology was not formally determined as a "coherent, logical, necessary system of general ideas." His theology, nevertheless, was by no means unstructured. It received its structure from a central interpretive theme, the justification of the sinner.

As will be seen below in the discussion of the history of the usage of the term, there is nothing to suggest that theology in either of the two senses above is more valid than the other. It becomes a problem only when there is lack of clarity about what is meant by theology, which, unfortunately, is very frequently the case. The purpose of the proposed definition is to make it possible to clarify how theology is understood in each of these cases, or what meanings are included, by showing how they relate to theology in the sense of the definition.

Conclusion

Thus we may conclude that what appeared to have been an obvious subject of reflection, the theology of the New Testament, is in fact extremely vague. It is something to which the Christian church did not give specific attention for many centuries, and now that the church has reflected on it for more than four centuries, there is very little agreement on the precise subject matter of such a theology. A look into the New Testament itself, in any case, does not reveal anything that could be considered with any degree of obviousness as a theology. Thus, it is also still not clear whether it is contained in the New Testament writings themselves or whether it is an underlying unity which has to be discerned by the interpreter, as Kümmel seems to suggest. And when it is assumed to be contained in the New Testament, there is no agreement on where it is to be found: only in Paul and John (Bultmann), or in the first three Gospels and the rest of the New Testament as well (Kümmel, Bonsirven). Furthermore, there is no agreement whether there are a number of theologies contained in it, for example, of Paul and of John (Bultmann), or a single theology for which there are a number of witnesses (Kümmel). Finally, it became clear that the term *theology* is not used unambiguously. It means one thing when used in relation to the New Testament as a whole, and something else when used in connection with something more specific within it, for example, the theology of

Paul (Kümmel) or the theology of a maturing Christianity (Bonsirven). A definition of theology was proposed as a possible means of clarifying the ways in which theology was understood by the authors to be discussed below.

B. THE ORIGIN OF NEW TESTAMENT THEOLOGY

1. The Origin and Nature of Christian Theology

As we have seen, theology as such is not obviously present in the New Testament. It may be presumed to be present at the deeper levels of the texts, but the texts themselves do not present an *obvious* theology, as even a cursory survey of their contents reveals. The only author whose writings reveal something that might come close to being a theology in the stricter sense is Paul, inasmuch as he does have a tendency to argue his point in a way that reveals the influence of the Cynic and Stoic philosophers of his time. The truths imparted by all other New Testament writings, including John's Gospel, are of an aphoristic nature, that is, they do not try to persuade by *reasoning*, but call for *recognition* of the validity of what is said. They might more properly be understood as having a claim to wisdom rather than to knowledge.

Paul's Letters, of course, at least invite reflection which might result in a theology. But they do not yet constitute theological literature in the sense of being either products of or presenting anything that even approximates a coherent system of thought on matters concerning the divine. Paul's reasoning in each case is ad hoc, serving the immediate pastoral and apostolic concerns of a particular occasion and audience, and that is true for his Letter to the Romans too. In any case, it cannot be argued reasonably that Christian theology is the product of a continuation of a process of thought that was started by Paul, much as some of his theological arguments might lend themselves to further reflection and possibly even to the development of such a theology.

From where then did Christian theology originate? It is worth noting that although the term *theology* and its cognates did occur in pre-Christian Greek thought, it was not used in the sense of disciplined thinking on matters concerning the divine. The earliest usage may be that of Plato in the *Republic* (379A),[6] where it denotes the composition of myths by the poets and is specifically distinguished from philosophy, in this case the philosophy of the founders of the

---

6. Cf. Gerhard Ebeling, "Theologie I: Begriffsgeschichtlich," in *Die Religion in Geschichte und Gegenwart*, ed. Kurt Galling, 3d ed. (Tübingen: J. C. B. Mohr [Paul Siebeck], 1957), vol. 1, col. 754.

ideal city-state: "It is appropriate for the founders of the city to know the regulations under which the poets should articulate myths, and not to allow them to deviate from these, but it is not appropriate for them (the founders themselves) to compose myths" (379A). In the very next sentence the composition of myths is referred to as "theology." This is then also, in general, the way in which the term *theology* and its cognates were used by the Greeks.

Although the Greeks did not use the term *theology* in the sense of disciplined thinking on matters concerning the divine, such disciplined thinking was, of course, not absent in Greek thought, as is very well known. Usage of the term *theology* for this type of thinking, however, is a development in Christianity, and a gradual one at that. It is only in Scholasticism that this understanding of theology as a coherent, logical, necessary system of thought is generally accepted. In the early Christian usage, the Greek meaning of theology as mythmaking remained influential, but in the course of the development of Christian thought the term acquired a variety of other meanings until it reached the abovementioned one, that is, of disciplined thinking concerning God, in Scholasticism.[7]

Notwithstanding that the term *theology* in the sense of disciplined thinking on matters concerning the divine does not go back to the Greeks, Christian thought did not develop without the decisive influence of the discipline of Greek thought, which is to say, philosophy. The *material* source from which the emerging Christian theology drew was the biblical revelation. But the *formal* discipline in which its thought was cast was derived from philosophy. Paul, along with other biblical writers, may have provided the material out of which Christian theology drew; they were the sources of revelation, but they did not provide the principles of disciplined thought by means of which it functioned. Christian theology through the Middle Ages did not try to think the thoughts of the biblical writers *as distinct from their own*. They thought their own thoughts, which they took for granted as being in continuity with those of the biblical writers. A double continuity was presumed: the material on which Christian thought was based had been provided by the biblical writers, and the tradition of the ongoing life and thought of the church bridged the historical gap separating the Bible from contemporary Christianity.

2. Contemporaneity of the Bible and the Living Religion in the Middle Ages

Medieval Christianity did not take note of the historical distance

7. Cf. ibid., cols. 754–64.

separating the Bible from the living faith, just as Israel disregarded a similar historical distance in Deuteronomy when Moses announced to the people ready to enter the promised land: "Jahweh, our God, made a covenant with us at Horeb; not with our fathers did he make this covenant, but with us, the living; all of us who are here today" (Deut. 5:2–3). This absence of historical distinction is most clearly revealed in medieval art where biblical scenes were presented in contemporary settings and dress, even with some contemporary personages appearing next to the biblical characters. The Bible was taken as contemporary, as an integral part of the living religion.

3. Historical Separation and Biblical Thought in the Reformation

All of that changed as a result of the Reformation and the Reformers' insistence on Scripture as the sole basis and norm for all Christian life and thought. The Reformers, of course, intended to establish the Bible's authority more firmly, completely, and immediately as the basis and norm over and against the contemporary church, as the means by which her abuses could be judged and corrected and by which Christendom could thus be renewed. However, that implied the rejection of the tradition of the ongoing life of the church and with it the continuity with the Bible which had been provided by it. The Bible was no longer an integral, contemporary part of the living religion but was separated from it by an intervening history, that very history of the ongoing life of the church which had previously provided continuity with the Bible. A historical consciousness thus arose with the Reformation. This was not immediately recognized, but it was only a question of time before it began to become clear, and historical criticism would emerge.

The rejection of tradition also meant that Christian theology could no longer think its own thoughts. If it was recognized that the Bible was not an integral, contemporaneous part of the living religion but was separated from it historically, it followed that theology also had to distinguish between contemporary thinking and that of the Bible. That is, Christianity could no longer think its own thoughts as if they were identical with the Bible's thoughts. It could no longer merely draw the material for its thinking from the Bible. It had to think the very thoughts of the biblical writers rather than its own and to interpret the former as they related to the contemporary life of the church, as had been done in an exemplary way by Luther and Calvin in their commentaries and in a more systematic way by Calvin in *The Institutes of the Christian Religion*. This is the way in which they tried to provide an immediacy with the Bible despite the historical distance, by an attentive listening to what it said, which meant a binding to the actual words, not a search for hidden meanings behind the words as in an allegorical interpretation.

4. The Dilemma of Christian Theology

That Christian theology could no longer think its own thought but had to think the thoughts of the biblical writers implied that theology had to be biblical and that its thoughts could no longer be subject to the formal discipline derived from philosophy. Also *formally* it had to be somehow grounded in the Bible. Luther tried to achieve this by grounding his thinking in what he considered the central theme in the Bible, the justification of the sinner, and by refusing to build on this a new "coherent, logical, necessary system" of theology. Lutheran orthodoxy, however, on the basis of this theme as its central idea, did build such a system. The development in Calvinism was similar.

The construction of such theological systems in Protestantism, while maintaining at the same time the conviction that theology had to be not only based on the Bible but grounded in it, produced what may be one of the most serious dilemmas in Christian thought: The Bible by its very nature could not provide the formal categories of thought on which a theological system could be built. Therefore the formal discipline of thought derived from philosophy could not be surrendered. But that discipline of thought was alien to the Bible.

And Catholicism, even though it did not accept the principle of "Scripture alone," did accept the principle, now explicitly stated, that theology had to be grounded in the Bible. Thus, it too became caught up in the dilemma of having to reconcile a theology, which received its formal categories of thought from philosophy, with the Bible, which was alien to these categories. [GK vs. HEB]

Nowhere is this dilemma expressed more succinctly than in the designation "biblical theology," or distinctively "Old Testament theology" and "New Testament theology," as long as theology continues to be understood in some sense as disciplined thought on matters concerning God in the sense of a coherent, logical, necessary system. It is the fact of this dilemma which leaves so much unclarity about what is involved in a biblical or an Old Testament or New Testament theology.

In fairness to the Reformation, it should be observed that it did not create these problems. They were inherent in the assumption that the Bible was the basis of Christian thought. In a sense, the Reformation merely exposed the difficulties of that assumption by insisting on being consistent about it. With regard to the Bible, the Reformation wanted more: a more complete anchoring of Christianity in the authority of the Bible. The developments which resulted from that insistence revealed that there was less: that theology could not be completely grounded in the Bible as long as it was conceived of as *Key* disciplined thought on matters concerning God in the sense derived from Greek philosophy.

5. The Bible as the Object of Critical Investigation

By placing the Bible over and against contemporary Christianity as a means of judging and renewing it, the Reformation in principle also established the inverse possibility. The distance which had been established between the Bible and its contemporary readers provided the precise requirement which made it possible for the readers, if they were courageous enough, to set themselves up over against the Bible, not necessarily with irreverence, and to subject it to critical investigation. This possibility was realized in a consistent way for the first time by Richard Simon (1638–1712), a Catholic priest who was expelled from his order for his efforts.

To begin with, Simon had already investigated the Old Testament and the New Testament as separate entities. He first wrote *A Critical History of the Old Testament* in 1678, but the largest part of it was destroyed before publication at the instigation of the influential Jacques-Benigne Bossuet. But then, in a series of works on the text, the translations, and the principle commentators of the New Testament, published between 1689 and 1695, Simon investigated the origin of the New Testament as a text in terms of its literary history and its transmission. Simon's work showed that the Bible was not as solid and self-explanatory as Protestants assumed when they made it the sole base and norm of Christian life and thought, but he was equally concerned that Catholics should take the biblical text as seriously as the Protestants had done. Although today recognized as the father of critical introduction to the Old Testament and the New Testament by Protestants and Catholics alike, Simon was rejected by both in his own time.

Simon already came to a number of critical insights that are still recognized today, for example, that the Gospel headings did not originate from the authors of the Gospels and that Mark 16:9–20 and John 7:53–8:11, the so-called longer ending of Mark and the pericope of the adulterous woman, do not occur in many of the earliest Greek manuscripts. His most significant and lasting contribution, however, is not such detailed insights but that he showed once and for all that the Bible could be the object of critical investigation. With that, one of the implications of the Reformation principle of "Scripture alone" was firmly established and historical criticism was on its way.

6. The Concern for the Bible in Lutheran Orthodoxy and in Pietism

The first biblical "theologies" did not originate as systematic presentations of the thoughts of the biblical writers, but as collections of passages from the Bible, in which in most cases texts from the Old Testament and the New Testament were juxtaposed indiscriminately. It was assumed that the various doctrines or dogmas were expressed in these passages, that is, the doctrines and dogmas on which Lutheran orthodoxy based its system.

The first such biblical theology appears to have been a work by Wolfgang Jacob Christmann, *Teutsche Biblische Theologie* (German Biblical Theology), published in 1629. Unfortunately, no extant copy of this work seems to have come down to us. The oldest existing copy of such a theology is Henricus A. Diest's *Theologica biblica,* published in 1643. It is a typical example of these theologies: a collection of texts under the headings of twenty-three doctrines, for example, concerning God, redemption, the Person of Christ, and so on, each with further subheadings, covering the entire scope of the dogmatic theology of the time.

The assumption on which these theologies were based was undoubtedly that the Reformation doctrines were grounded in the Bible and that these collections of texts were means of ensuring that these doctrines remain attuned to it, apart from underscoring their biblical nature and authority. In this way the authors of these theologies tried to remain true to the original Reformation principles. The Reformers had proceeded in their thinking on the basis of the Bible, but now a system of dogmatic theology had developed in Protestantism, and the authors of these theologies were looking at the Bible from the point of view of that dogmatic system and trying to make the Bible the basis of the system, a direct inversion of the approach of the Reformers. Their theologies were not systematic presentations of the thoughts of the biblical writers, as for example, Calvin had tried to do in his *Institutes,* but the dogmatic theology of Lutheran orthodoxy expressed by means of biblical texts. They were neither truly biblical nor, strictly speaking, theologies, since they were really grounded in orthodox theology and not in the Bible and were mere collections of biblical texts which were intended to underscore an already existing dogmatic theology.

A completely negative reaction against Lutheran dogmatic theology came from the pietists. Their concern was expressed succinctly by Philipp Jacob Spener in his Pia Desideria (1675), in which he recounts how Scholastic theology had been thrown out the front door by Luther but was let in again through the back door by others (meaning orthodox theologians) only to be thrown out again by the evangelical, that is, pietist churches, which reintroduced the true biblical theology.[8] The "true biblical theology" for Spener meant simply an openness to the Bible without the influence of dogmatics.

Notwithstanding their very different reactions to dogmatic theology, the orthodox authors of the biblical theologies and pietists alike were concerned to maintain the fundamental Reformation principle that the basis and norm of all Christian life and thought had to be the Bible. The difference in their approaches indicates different mindsets. The pietists were opposed to all thought that was subject to formal discipline of a philosophical type, because they sensed it to be alien to the Bible. They themselves, of course, had a formal principle of their own determining their thinking and also their reading of Scripture, namely, the centrality of the progression of the individual from sinfulness to rebirth as a new creature before God.

Orthodoxy, similarly concerned about the Bible as basis and norm of all Christian thought, was not willing to surrender the already formulated dogmatic theology. By means of their collections of biblical texts, they hoped to have been able to maintain both, the Bible as basis and norm of theology as well as the already formulated dogmatic theology. However, because the biblical texts were collected under the ordering principles of dogmatic theology and were thus merely expressions of that theology by means of biblical texts, they did not really return to a grounding in the Bible. In order to do that, a reversal of the roles of basis and superstructure would have been necessary—if the intention of the Reformers was to have been carried out while maintaining the possibility of a dogmatic theology. An attempt at doing exactly that was to be the major contribution of Johann Philipp Gabler (1753–1826).

Conclusion

Thus it appears that although the term *theology* in what has become its more technical meaning did not originate from the Greeks but is a product of Christian thought, Christian theology did not develop without the decisive influence of the formal discipline of thought in Greek philosophy. In Scholasticism through the Middle

---

8. Philipp Jacob Spener, *Pia Desideria*, ed. Kurt Aland, in Hans Lietzmann, gen. ed., *Kleine Texte für Vorlesungen und Übungen*, no. 170 (Berlin: Walter de Gruyter, 1940, 1952), p. 26; English translation, *Pia Desideria*, translated, edited, and with an introduction by Theodore G. Tappert (Philadelphia: Fortress Press, 1964).

Ages, however, it was taken for granted that theology was fully in continuity with the Bible, which was assumed to have been an integral part of contemporary Christian life and thought and which provided the material on which theology was based. These assumptions came to be questioned fundamentally by the Reformation principle of Scripture alone as the basis of Christian life and thought. By placing the Bible over and against contemporary Christian life and thought as the means of renewing it, however, the Reformers by implication made it possible to make the Bible in turn the object of critical investigation and so made possible the rise of historical criticism.

The first so-called biblical theologies were neither truly biblical nor in the strict sense theologies but formulations of an already existing orthodox Lutheran theology by means of collections of biblical texts. The basis of these collections was not biblical thought but the orthodox theology which was brought to expression by means of them. The *fundamental* identity of the collections was with orthodox theology, not with biblical thought. The authors of these "theologies," nevertheless, like the pietists, were concerned to reaffirm the Bible as the sole base of theology. Such a concern, however, could not have been realized unless the roles of basis and superstructure were once more reversed to what they had been at the time of the Reformation, with the Bible once more fulfilling the role of basis, and theology that of superstructure. That was the task which Gabler was going to try to accomplish.

II
Biblical Theology as Part of a Comprehensive Theological Task: Johann Philipp Gabler

1. Antecedents to the Achievement of Gabler

Two developments during the second half of the eighteenth century prepared the way for the decisive breakthrough in biblical theology marked by Johann Philipp Gabler's inaugural address at Altdorf on 30 March 1787: *(a)* the distinction made by Johann Salomo Semler (1725–91) between the word of God revealed in Scripture and the words of Scripture themselves, and *(b)* the argument by Gotthilf Traugott Zachariä (1729–77) that biblical theology was not to be found in the biblical writings themselves but had to be derived from them.

According to Semler the word of God was to be found in Scripture but was not identical with it. This differentiation freed the Bible for critical investigation without necessarily creating a conflict with the revelation contained in it. Similarly, Semler distinguished between religion and theology, making it possible for the latter to develop as a critical discipline, free from the actual engagement in the practice of religion.

For Zachariä the task of a biblical theology was to investigate which theological conceptions were common to the biblical writings, that is, which conceptions were not bound to the particular historical circumstances of the individual writings. This implied a recognition that the Bible was not only separated historically from the contemporary reader but that it was itself subject to the contingencies of history. Only what transcended these contingencies could be considered unchanging and thus the appropriate material for a biblical theology. Zachariä set himself to the task of identifying that material in his *Biblische Theologie* (Biblical Theology), published, partly posthumously, between 1771 and 1786. The subtitle, "An Investigation of the Biblical Basis for the Most Important

Theological Doctrines," clarifies its purpose but also reveals the degree to which it was still bound by the procedures of the orthodox biblical theologies. Nevertheless, he "investigated" the biblical texts rather than merely using them to express already formulated doctrines, as had been done in the orthodox theologies. Thus it is not surprising that Gabler was so heavily indebted to him, an indebtedness which Gabler explicitly recognized more than once in his inaugural address. In a sense Gabler merely thought through what Zachariä had been trying to accomplish. His main interest throughout, like that of Zachariä, was in the stable, unchanging ideas contained in the biblical writings as a basis for dogmatic theology.

2. Distinguishing between the Various Theological Disciplines

Johann Philipp Gabler is generally credited with having established biblical theology as a separate discipline, independent of dogmatic theology. This was an important contribution indeed, but to mention it alone is one-sided to the point of distortion. The establishment of biblical theology as an independent discipline was achieved by Gabler within the framework of a larger enterprise, that is, that of distinguishing between the various aspects of the theological task as a whole, providing a separate discipline to take care of each of these aspects, and defining the limits of these disciplines as well as the interrelationships between them. His main objective had been to insure that the Bible was reestablished as the basis of all theology, with a biblically based dogmatic theology as its crown and final achievement. Indeed, his ultimate concern was to arrive at a proper dogmatic theology, firmly established on the biblical foundation which was to be provided by biblical theology. The establishment of an independent biblical theology, thus, was not an end in itself but part and parcel of a larger concern for theology as a whole.

This distinguishing of the various aspects of the theological task and of the disciplines to take care of them was made within an even larger framework, that is, that of the distinction between religion and theology. The work of Gabler, thus, may be characterized in terms of three major distinctions: between religion and theology, between biblical and dogmatic theology, and, as will be seen below, between biblical theology in a broader and in a narrower sense.

The program for carrying out these distinctions was outlined in his inaugural address when he assumed his professorship in Altdorf on 30 March 1787: "Address Concerning the True Distinction between Biblical and Dogmatic Theology, and the Correct Definition of Their Purposes." It was the program for everything he subsequently did on biblical theology, but in many ways it was also the program for all that was accomplished since then on the subject. In the meantime much has been clarified and thought through in more detail, but there is scarcely an achievement that cannot be considered as in some sense a carrying out of Gabler's program. Even more, the clarity that had been achieved by him was lost in the subsequent developments and was never again equalled.

3. The Problem of the Biblical Foundation of Theology

The most fundamental distinction for Gabler, thus, was between religion and theology. He understood the Bible to have contained not theology but religion, that is, a divine teaching handed down in writing. Religion was an ordinary, simple way of understanding. Theology was subtle, highly developed. As a way of understanding, thus, theology and religion stood over against each other, but theology was nevertheless supposed to have been based on religion. In the previous attempts to ensure this grounding of theology in the biblical religion—by making direct use of the biblical material in the so-called biblical theologies of orthodoxy—the biblical material inevitably functioned merely to give expression to the existing doctrines of dogmatic theology. Gabler, however, argued that if the Bible was to be reestablished as the sole basis of theology, it would have to be investigated by a discipline that was independent of dogmatic theology, with accountability only to the biblical material which it had to interpret. That was to be an entirely new discipline, biblical theology, which had little more than the name in common with the earlier biblical theologies of orthodoxy.

4. The Purpose of Biblical Theology

However, since the intention was that the Bible was to be reestablished as the basis of all of theology, this new independent discipline of biblical theology could not remain an end in itself. Its ultimate task was to mediate between biblical religion and dogmatic theology by making it possible for the former to function as the basis for the latter. Biblical theology was eminently qualified for such a task since it shared in both biblical religion and dogmatic theology. Its subject matter was the biblical religion but its methodology was theological as the means by which it transformed the biblical religion into a theological system which could form the (biblical) basis for dogmatic theology.

This is a point of very great significance. In the subsequent development the independence of biblical theology from dogmatic theology was emphasized one-sidedly, that is, at the cost of forgetting its mediating function between the biblical religion and dogmatic theology. Biblical theology came to be understood very much as an end in itself, with the result that it was no longer clearly distinguished from dogmatic theology. In this way, inadvertently, dogmatic interests once more gained a foothold in biblical theology, or in Old Testament and New Testament theology as separate disciplines. The clarity of Gabler was lost.

Similarly, in contemporary dogmatics (systematic theology in the current, narrower sense) theologians make use of the Bible in a way which differs only superficially from that of orthodoxy. Of course, no contemporary dogmatic theologian attempts to express his or her theology by means of a compendium of biblical texts. Nevertheless, like orthodoxy, their usage of Scripture may be more a reaffirmation of already well-formed dogmas than the development of dogmas on the basis of a thorough investigation of the biblical religion.

The refusal to accept a division of labor in theology—or a clear distinction of tasks when more than one is performed by a single scholar—has consistently resulted in confusion and in a failure to accomplish either of the tasks in a satisfactory way. The greatest blame for this state of affairs may rest on the biblical theologians. By their obsession with independence in the performance of their task and, accordingly, claiming the entire theological enterprise for themselves, they do not provide by design a basis for dogmatic theology— and then they are annoyed when they are almost completely ignored by dogmatic theology.

5. *Theology as a Comprehensive Systematic Task*

By means of his distinctions between the various theological disciplines, Gabler was able to define every aspect of systematic theology as a comprehensive task, beginning with a systematic description of the biblical religion in which equal attention was given to all concepts, including those that were contingent—biblical theology in the broader sense; moving then to an identification of the contingent concepts and eliminating them from further consideration to leave only a system of the unchanging concepts as the basis for dogmatic theology—biblical theology in the narrower sense; turning finally to the philosophizing about all matters that related to the divine on the basis of the foundation provided by biblical theology in the narrower sense—dogmatic theology. He subsequently called biblical theology in the broader sense *true*, and in the narrower sense *pure* biblical theology, because the former had to be *true* to the biblical religion in every respect, whereas the latter concerned only the unchanging concepts, *purified* of those that were contingent.

What Gabler's distinctions and definitions of the various aspects of the theological task fundamentally accomplished was to clarify the limits of expectation in each discipline and to prevent confusion of one disciplinary task with another. The basic confusion in his time was that the biblical theologies of orthodoxy were in reality dogmatic theologies in disguise, not intentionally but inadvertently. Theology which, according to the Reformers, had to perform a critical task for the life of the church, judging and renewing it, had become a mere affirmation of various Lutheran doctrines. Everything had become turned upside down, with dogmatics instead of the Bible forming the base of theological thinking—against all good intentions. Gabler wanted to turn things right side up again, with the Bible reestablished as the foundation of all theology. It cannot be emphasized strongly enough that this had been his real intention, rather than to establish specifically a biblical theology as a discipline independent of dogmatics. Biblical theology was intended for a specific purpose, that is, to serve dogmatic theology by providing it with an independent base. With regard to its purpose, thus, biblical theology was not independent of dogmatic theology. If biblical theology completed its task successfully, dogmatic theology too would be able to accomplish its intended purpose. It would desist from reaffirming existing church doctrines and would develop doctrines on the biblical foundation provided by biblical theology. In that way it would be able to contribute to church renewal rather than sanction stagnation.

6. The Foundation of Dogmatic Theology Not Subject to Critical Scrutiny

What disturbed Gabler most of all was the lack of a factor of stability in theology, as was demonstrated by the large number of very different theologies of Scholasticism and also of Lutheran theologians. He was convinced that the Bible did not lend itself to such variety; rather, the reason for this variety was to be found in the theologies themselves. The biblical religion as divine teaching was stable, but somewhere in the development of theology on the presumed basis of the divine biblical teaching, the stability was lost. Since the biblical teaching remained always the same, it could be expected that this would also be true of a biblical theology—if it was freed from the determination of dogmatics. But Gabler was also concerned that dogmatic theology should not be allowed to remain completely subject to change and thus uncertainty. Of course, dogmatic theology was to remain relevant to the continually changing situation of the church, and in that sense it had to keep changing in order to adapt itself to ever new tasks. However, notwithstanding this necessity of continual adaptation, Gabler was concerned that it should be based on a fundamental stability, that is, the stability provided by biblical theology in the form of the system of unchanging concepts derived from the Bible.

It should be noted, thus, that theology according to Gabler was not pure philosophy—a philosophy of religion—but philosophizing within the specific context of the biblical teaching handed down in Scripture. In this way certain limits were set for theology as Christian philosophy. All other human disciplines were constantly changing; everything was variable except, one might assume, the formal discipline of thought itself. The same applied also to theology, but in its case the change occurred within very specific limits, that is, the limits imposed by the biblical religion as the basis on which it philosophized. Gabler was concerned that in addition to the stability provided by the formal discipline of thought, there should be in theology also a material feature that was invariable, the biblical religion as presented systematically by biblical theology. In that way dogmatic theology too would participate in the stability provided by the biblical religion, not directly, but as mediated through biblical theology.

This might be best illustrated by reference to the problem of the founding events of the Christian religion. From a religious point of view, and through more than nineteen centuries of Christianity, it has been tacitly assumed that these events were historical. Historical criticism, however, as a method of theological inquiry shed doubt on the historicity of these events. This led to the very unfortunate distrust which has developed between the religious and the theological communities and to the crisis experienced by those who belong to both. This distrust and the resulting crisis occurred because it was not recognized that there was not only one, that is, the historical, approach to the "historicity" of these events. The religious approach was *fundamentally* different. The historical approach became absolutized, and the religious approach was taken to be indentical with it or, what may have been worse, subject to it.

From the historian's point of view, only events that can hold up under critical historical scrutiny can be considered historical. Everything is judged variable unless it fits into the invariable structure of the discipline of thought, in this case the discipline of historical inquiry. This is a fundamentally different approach from that of religion. From a religious point of view, commitment (or faith) does not depend on, nor can it wait for, the affirmation of the historicity of the founding events by the historian. This holds true irrespective of whether such faith derives from the Christian religion, a mystery religion, or some other religion. From the point of view of religion, critical judgments about historicity are unnecessary because the events as described are either apprehended as significant or they are not.

It is precisely the historical-critical investigation of Christianity which should have been able to establish that the approaches of history and of religion to these founding events were fundamentally different. It should have been able to show that in the religious approach events were *tacitly assumed* to be historical, which could have been wrong from a strictly historical point of view, without the religious faith being aware of its possible error in judgment. Historical inquiry should have accepted this as a characteristic difference in the religious approach instead of trying to impose its own approach on religion. What makes this imposition particularly intolerable is that it includes the judgment that the validity of a religion depends on the historical verification of the founding events, a judgment which is so pervasive that it is taken to be self-evident—even by believers! This is a fundamental self-misconception of the religious approach.

From a Christian religious point of view, thus, the founding events are tacitly assumed to be historical. They do not need critical verification. To give up this assumption would mean to surrender the fundamental religious conviction and to assume the point of view of the historian. Religious understanding is not subject to historical verification of the founding events. It proceeds from the apprehension of the events as significant, which usually carries the secondary *tacit* assumption that they actually happened. In that way limits were set for religion and for religious thought. These limits have to be acknowledged if religion is to remain religion and not to become transformed into something else, for example, a history or, under other circumstances, a philosophy of religion.

Gabler intended something similar for dogmatic theology. According to him, dogmatic theology did make use of the discipline of thought of philosophy, but on the firm basis set for it by biblical theology, that is, a basis over which it could have no control. The task of dogmatic theology was to think through all matters that related to the divine, but it had to do so on the basis of the foundation provided for it by biblical theology. It was not possible for dogmatic theology to inquire into that basis itself. For dogmatic theology the basis was invariable, and in that sense it participated in the religious commitment through the mediation of biblical theology.

7. The Mediating Function of Biblical Theology

Gabler's argument for the independence of biblical theology from dogmatic theology clearly was not motivated by a narrow concern for biblical theology as such but by an attempt to understand the theological task as a whole. He not only established the independence of biblical theology as the only way in which it could accomplish its task properly; he also clarified the way in which alone dogmatic theology could accomplish its task as a critical, philosophical discipline with the task of continually judging and renewing the church by developing doctrines that were relevant for the particular situations in which it found itself. The *independence* of biblical theology was established *in relationship*, on the one hand, to the Bible and, on the other, to dogmatic theology in such a way that each could function with maximum effectiveness in the accomplishment of its distinctive task.

8. The Distinction between Religion and Theology

The most basic distinction for Gabler, thus, was between religion and theology. It was a distinction which he took over from earlier scholars, including Semler. Religion was an ordinary, plain way of understanding. Theology was subtle, highly sophisticated. What was contained in the Bible was religion, not theology. It was a divine teaching handed down in writing of what every Christian had to know, believe, and do to have eternal life.

Theology was developed by human ability and the human mind, drawing its information not only from the Bible but also from other areas, especially from philosophy and history. It originated from careful and constant observation of all the relevant phenomena and thus had many interrelationships with other disciplines. It was concerned not only with matters within the area of the Christian religion but also with everything that had a relationship to the latter, clarifying all such matters with great care and comprehensiveness. In this way theology provided for dialectical thoroughness and exactness. In short, theology for Gabler was Christian philosophy, a philosophy about all matters that related to the Christian religion.

It should be noted, however, that religion, as he understood it, was a teaching and a way of understanding. He conceived of it very much in terms of ideas. The difference between religion and theology, thus, was not between practice and thought. Both had to do with thoughts and understanding, but the former was plain and transparent, the latter complex, requiring great effort of mind.

With all of that, however, the real point of the distinction has not yet been reached. Gabler was persuaded that religion concerned fundamentally what was unchanging, divine, whereas theology concerned what was constantly changing, human. Thus, even though he recognized that also in the Bible there were conceptions that were intended by divine decree(!) to be binding only for a certain time, a certain place, or a certain type of people, such as the Mosaic rituals or Paul's insistence that women should go veiled, the task of a biblical theology was to discern these and to eliminate them from further consideration in order that only those concepts that remain, the unchanging, divine concepts, would form the firm base for theological reflection. One gets the very distinct impression that these contingent conceptions in the Bible were merely concessions to particular human situations. In that regard they may be considered similar to dogmatic theology, which had the specific task of relating the unchanging, divine concepts to particular human situations.

What concerned Gabler at the most fundamental level were the unchanging, divine concepts in the Bible. One would probably not go wrong if one assumes that for him only the unchanging concepts were really divine. Those which applied to particular situations were concessions to the human condition and, thus, not pure expressions of divine revelation.

Thus, Gabler was confronted with the contradiction between the unchanging, divine revelation in the form of the biblical religion, on the one hand, and an ever changing theology in the form of a variety of very different "theologies," on the other. Theology was of necessity contingent, but it should have had at least the constancy of being based on the firm, unchanging base of the biblical religion. The Bible did not lend itself to a variety of different theologies. Rather the differences were inherent in the theologies themselves. To be sure, there were a number of obscure passages in the Bible, and they induced interpreters to foist their own views on the Bible. In such cases the Bible became a mere tool for theologies. This situation had to be changed in order that the Bible could once more exert a decisive influence on theology, as the Reformers had demanded. Christian theology should be based on the Bible, and this was obviously not the case at the time, as he saw it.

The problem was that the Bible *as such* could not provide a base for theology since it was itself not a theology but a collection of religious writings which were themselves subject to interpretation. What was needed was a discipline that could mediate between the biblical religion and dogmatic theology. That was the task to be performed by biblical theology. The assumption was that such a biblical theology would be able to abstract a foundation from the

Bible on which dogmatic theology could be based. Such a foundation would obviously have to be a theological, that is, systematic presentation of the unchanging religious teaching contained in the Bible. If such a biblical theology were to function properly it would have to be independent from all outside influence, especially from dogmatic theology for which it had to provide the foundation. Only in that way would it be able to present an accurate picture of the biblical religion.

In Gabler's distinction between religion and theology one can sense the concerns of the pietists (religion) as well as of orthodoxy (theology). He affirmed the validity of both: the concern for the ordinary, plain religion of the Bible with the pietists, as well as the refinement and precision of theology with orthodoxy. By distinguishing clearly between these, and so defining the function and limits of each, he was able to move to a position beyond both pietism and orthodoxy in which he could affirm religion as well as theology. By clearly defining the limits of each, it was possible to avoid confusing them and expecting the one to perform the task of the other or allowing the one to impinge on the function of the other. Theology becomes a problem only when it is mistaken for religion. When the tasks of each were clearly defined in this way, there was no reason why they should be in conflict with each other.

What is particularly noteworthy about Gabler's distinction is that it provided a perfectly appropriate place for the human endeavor, for philosophy, in theology without surrendering any of the ground of the biblical religion which was of such fundamental concern to the pietists. In that regard, however, he probably went further than even most orthodox theologians might have been willing to go.

9. The Distinction between Biblical and Dogmatic Theology

In order to ascertain for the Bible its proper place as the basis of Christian thought, and specifically of theology, thus, Gabler required the mediation of a biblical theology that was independent of the influence of dogmatic theology. It was this concern which called for "the true distinction between biblical and dogmatic theology and for the correct discrimination of their purposes," as expressed in the title of his inaugural address. Biblical theology had the task of presenting in a systematic way the pure,[9] unchanging, divine concepts contained in the Bible as the basis for dogmatic theology. Dogmatic

9. The term *pure* strikes us as somewhat unusual today. Gabler undoubtedly used it in the sense in which it was used by his contemporary, Immanuel Kant, for example, in *The Critique of Pure Reason*. Thus, a biblical theology which was comprehensible by pure reason.

theology, on the other hand, consisted of the philosophizing about all matters concerning the divine on the basis provided by biblical theology.

What distinguished biblical and dogmatic theology, according to Gabler, was that the former was "historical," representing what the biblical writers thought about the divine, whereas the latter was "didactic," teaching everything that could be thought about matters relating to the divine on the basis of what was presented by the former. Dogmatic theology was contingent, subject as it was to the ability of the theologian, his or her geographic and historical circumstances, determination by the church denomination or school of thought to which he or she belonged, and so on. Since the task of dogmatic theology was by its very nature tied in with such circumstances, contingency was built into it. Biblical theology, in contrast, was stable, having as its material the unchanging teaching of the Bible.

Since the biblical writings themselves, however, were also subject to certain contingencies, there was a sense in which they were historical in the same way as dogmatic theology was, that is, in the sense of historical contingency. What Gabler had in mind in identifying biblical theology as historical in distinction from dogmatic theology was that the subject matter of the former, that is, the biblical revelation, was a fixed body of material from the past, whereas the subject matter of dogmatic theology, which included everything that had a relationship to the Christian religion, was constantly changing.

Clearly, the distinction which Gabler made between religion and theology was strictly a distinction between specifically dogmatic theology and (the biblical) religion. Biblical theology was something in between, participating in both. Its subject matter was the unchanging biblical teaching, which was a religion, but its task was to present this subject matter in a systematic way, not as a religion but as a theology. It was that feature of biblical theology which enabled it to mediate between the biblical religion and dogmatic theology.

10. The Distinction between True Biblical Theology and Pure Biblical Theology

However, since the Bible contained not only unchanging, divine teaching but also conceptions that had been intended only for particular times, places, and types of peoples, biblical theology had to distinguish between these conceptions and the unchanging divine teaching. Since the former were themselves subject to change, they could not be included in what constituted a firm biblical foundation for dogmatic theology. On the other hand, to try to separate out the contingent and unchanging concepts before a complete picture of the biblical religion had been presented could only lead to a distortion. For that reason Gabler made the further distinction between biblical theology in a broader and in a narrower sense. As has already been indicated, he called the former true and the latter pure biblical theology.

Biblical theology in the broader sense had the task of systematically collecting and ordering all the conceptions concerning the divine in the Bible, also those that were not explicitly present but could be inferred by a comparision of more than one passage. It had to produce a fully comprehensive system of biblical theology, a *true* picture of the biblical religion. In order to accomplish this task satisfactorily, Gabler further distinguished two separate phases in which it was to be performed. The first was very much what we know today as a thorough historical-critical interpretation of the biblical writings, Old and New Testament separately, but also giving individual attention to the various biblical writers. He was very much concerned that one should not stop at the surface meanings of a text. So, for example, if one discovered that an author gave expression to the same matter in different ways in more than one passage, these passages should be compared in order to be able to distinguish between the surface expressions and the underlying meaning. Even in this biblical theology in the broader sense Gabler was concerned with general ideas.

The second phase was to identify all the general concepts and to order them, giving close attention to differences due to the particular historical, geographic, and religious settings to which they belonged. The object was to produce a comprehensive system of biblical theology. As a model for such a system, Gabler commended the system of Stoic thought which had been produced by a certain Tiedemann. What Gabler had in mind was not a mere historical *re*presentation of the biblical religion but a systematic *presentation* of it in such a way that one could understand what it had been all about as an historical phenomenon. It should be noted that this was not yet a theology but a systematic historical presentation of the biblical religion. That is then also the way in which it was going to be understood, for example, by Adolf Deissmann and by William Wrede.

Biblical theology in the narrower sense, that is, pure biblical theology, had the task of presenting the unchanging biblical teaching which was valid for all times, purified of those concepts that were limited to particular circumstances. It had to proceed by first indentifying the latter concepts and then eliminating them from further consideration. The procedure was obviously not to try to collect the unchanging concepts from the comprehensive system immediately but, by a process of elimination, that is, of the contingent concepts, to let them emerge as the purified concepts that remained. He probably assumed that this would have been a more reliable procedure. The purified system of these unchanging, divine concepts would then have formed a firm foundation on which the philosophical reflection in dogmatic theology could take place.

If the comprehensive theological task was performed in this way, Gabler was confident, it would be possible to distinguish between the areas of divine and of human wisdom in dogmatic theology, between the unchanging biblical concepts provided by biblical theology and the human philosophizing on the basis of them. In that way the objective of a biblically based dogmatic theology would have been achieved.

11. The Significance of Gabler's Distinctions

The distinction which Gabler made between biblical theology in the broader and in the narrower sense may be considered as equal in importance to the distinction between dogmatic and biblical theology. It is equally important that the task of an historical presentation of the biblical religion in all its details be produced independently of the attempt to distinguish between what was contingent and what remained valid for all times. It has not always been perceived in that way. In his study of Gabler and Georg Lorenz Bauer, Otto Merk considers it as a distinct advantage in the work of Bauer that he included the *interpretation* of the meaning of biblical material in a single historical *reconstruction* of biblical theology, whereas Gabler needed his two separate disciplines to perform these tasks.[10] But one would think that it was precisely the distinction of these two tasks, coordinate with two separate disciplines, which could have ensured the possibility of progress in the accomplishment of both the historical-critical reconstruction of the Christian religion as well as the interpretation of its significance.

According to Merk, however, Gabler reveals substantial deficiencies in the carrying out of his program of biblical theology, specifically with regard to "historical biblical theology." Because of his objective to provide a basis for dogmatic theology, he remained within the limits of his time in his attempt to develop biblical theology as a discipline independent of dogmatics. Because of the intended "pure" biblical theology, important in his time, the

10.   Otto Merk, *Biblische Theologie des Neuen Testaments* (Marburg: N. G. Elwert Verlag, 1972), p. 202.

historical-critical task remained only half complete. Merk is aware that these "deficiencies" were grounded in Gabler's fundamental intention to establish a firm base for dogmatic theology.[11] The deficiencies, thus, are obviously to be found in the program itself, not in the carrying out of it.

It is true, of course, that Gabler was concerned with general concepts, not with historical particularity as such, even in his true biblical theology. That was, however, not so much due to his concern to provide a basis for dogmatic theology by means of his biblical theology as it was caused by the lack of a real appreciation for the particularities of history. Nevertheless, he insisted that nothing of the biblical religion should be left out of consideration in the presentation of it in a biblical theology in the broader sense, which encouraged and led to the recognition of the importance of historical particularity. Gabler's intention for biblical theology in the broader sense had been "purely historical," as none other than Ferdinand Christian Baur interpreted it in his lectures on New Testament theology. It was only a question of time before that intention was to be realized in the work of, among others, Baur himself. But in an even more thorough way the broader task of biblical theology was subsequently performed in the *Religionsgeschichtliche* (history of religions) school, as outlined programmatically for the New Testament by William Wrede and carried out by Wilhelm Bousset in *Kyrios Christos.*

There is a sense in which the narrower task was performed by the large number of biblical theologies that appeared since Gabler, separately for the most part, as Old Testament and New Testament theology. However, in these theologies the task of interpreting the lasting meaning of the Bible—or Old Testament and New Testament distinctively—was not distinguished from the broader task of a comprehensive, systematic, historical presentation of biblical religion.

What distinguishes the abovementioned theologies even more significantly from Gabler's biblical theology in the narrower sense is that they are not clearly distinguished from dogmatic theology. Because they are conceived of as independent of dogmatic theology in an absolute sense, they become ends in themselves. And since they are no longer means of providing dogmatic theology with a biblical base, aspects of dogmatic theology are incorporated into them. In this way dogmatic theology is once more provided with an avenue of influence on biblical theology. Ironically, it is the very fact that the

11. Ibid., p. 113.

independence from dogmatic theology is taken absolutely which provides this avenue to dogmatic theology.

Possibly the most important but also the most neglected feature of Gabler's distinction between biblical and dogmatic theology was not so much that he established the independence of the former from the latter but that he established it for the specific purpose of providing a firm biblical foundation on which dogmatic theology could be based. Biblical theology was freed from a *pre*determination by dogmatic theology but remained determined by it with regard to its purpose.

It should be noted that Gabler recognized correctly that also biblical theology, even the historical presentation of the history of the biblical religion in a true biblical theology, had to be systematic. From this it follows that the contemporary custom of using the designation "systematic theology" for the discipline to which Gabler referred with the traditional designation "dogmatic theology" is misleading. It would be more appropriate to retain the designation "dogmatic theology" or "dogmatics" for this discipline in the sense in which Gabler interpreted it. That would then also make it possible to substitute misleading designations such as "liberation theology" with the more appropriate "doctrine of liberation" as a very important part of a comprehensive system of dogmatic theology.

Gabler, thus, had broken with the Reformation demand that the Bible should be the *sole* base of theology. Theology was a philosophizing about all matters concerning the divine on the basis of the Bible. It was important for him, nevertheless, to distinguish in theology between the areas of human and divine wisdom. Furthermore, Gabler did not carry out the Reformers' demand that theology should be grounded on biblical thought itself. It was clear to him that theological and biblical thought were not of the same kind, the latter being religious. For that reason there had to be an intermediate discipline with the task of transforming the biblical religious thinking into the form of a theological system. In that way, by demanding less, Gabler was able to achieve more of what the Reformers had intended. By such a transformation he provided at least the possibility of biblical thought being the determining influence in theology.

Conclusion

The fundamentally most important distinction which Gabler made was between religion and theology. In order to mediate between the biblical religion and dogmatic theology there had to be a separate discipline, biblical theology, and because of the complexity of the task of mediation it was necessary to distinguish further between the systematic gathering and presentation of the biblical material and the differentiation of that part of the material that could serve as the basis of dogmatic theology, respectively, between true and pure biblical theology or between historical presentation and theological interpretation.

Gabler still understood the biblical religion very much in the sense of teachings, and in that he was followed by Ferdinand Christian Baur in his thoroughly historical interpretation of New Testament Christianity. In due course, however, consistency in the presentation of the history of the biblical religion—increasingly Old Testament and New Testament separately—was to reveal that there was more to a religion than teachings, that teachings were not even the most important aspect of a living religion. It was in the *Religionsgeschichtliche* school that the full implications of a true biblical theology were recognized, namely, that it was not a theology at all, but, with regard to the New Testament, the presentation of the history of the developing New Testament religion. The program for such a presentation was outlined by William Wrede and carried out with regard to a Christology by Wilhelm Bousset.

In the period after Gabler, attention was focused almost exclusively on a true biblical theology. Only much later, in the work of Rudolf Bultmann and his school, did the task of a pure biblical theology (of the New Testament) begin to receive serious attention. Before that task could be accomplished it was necessary for New Testament theology, particularly in the sense of pure biblical theology, to be freed from the contingent Enlightenment outlook in terms of which Gabler formulated his program.

III

New Testament Theology as the History of New Testament Religion: William Wrede and Wilhelm Bousset

INTRODUCTION

After Gabler it became increasingly normal to investigate Old Testament and New Testament theology separately. From here on, then, we will focus our attention only on the latter.

The next important step in the development of New Testament theology was marked by an essay *On the Task and Method of the So-called New Testament Theology* (1897) by William Wrede (1859–1906) in which he outlined a program for a history of the New Testament religion. In such a history, Gabler's program for a New Testament theology in the broader sense was to be carried out in a consistent way and certainly well beyond the limits that Gabler may have imagined. But prior to Wrede's programmatic essay there were at least two other developments worthy of mention: (1) the enactment of a thoroughly historical interpretation of the New Testament by Ferdinand Christian Baur (1792–1860), outlined with regard to a New Testament theology in the introduction to his posthumously published *Lectures on New Testament Theology* (1864) subheaded *Conception, History, and Plan of a New Testament Theology;* and (2) the recognition that the New Testament religion was not a teaching from which a system of general concepts could be derived, for example, by Adolf Deissmann (1866–1937) in his trial lecture before the faculty of theology of the University of Marburg on 9 August 1892, "Concerning the Method of the Biblical Theology of the New Testament."

A. ANTECEDENTS TO THE PROGRAM OF WREDE AND BOUSSET

1. New Testament Theology as History: Ferdinand Christian Baur

The name of Baur has become almost synonymous with a thoroughly historical interpretation of the New Testament. He did indeed understand the liberation of biblical theology from dogmatics in the sense of a thoroughly historical interpretation. The task of biblical theology was to present as clearly as possible the historical "as the essential element" of the Bible. For Baur the Bible did not merely contain a history. It was, so to speak, in its essence a history, and it was the task of a biblical theology to present it as such with the greatest possible clarity.

In the presentation of this history, the interpreter had to refrain from trying to discern what had value for, or was considered true by, him or her. One should ask such questions as little in the presentation of biblical history as one would with regard to the history of doctrine. Baur considered biblical history to have been the first phase of the history of doctrine. The task was to present what the biblical writers believed or considered true, irrespective of the interpreter's own opinion about it. Futhermore, an accurate biblical history could not be presented as long as the interpreter worked under the restraint of the assumption that the Bible contained nothing but revelation from beginning to end. Such an assumption could only serve to drive the interpreter into an apologetic attitude toward his or her subject matter.

This was in effect a radicalization of Gabler's distinction between a true and a pure biblical theology, even though Baur made no provision for the latter. In the presentation of biblical theology as history, the distinction between what was contingent and what was valid for all times had become irrelevant. On the other hand, Baur's lack of a distinction between New Testament history and theology amounted to a theologizing of history. The distinction between a historical presentation of the New Testament religion and something that could genuinely have been called a theology of the New Testament was given up.

An immediate consequence of Baur's emphasis on the importance of history itself was that the isolated presentation of the teachings of the biblical writers, individually next to each other, could no longer satisfy. It was necessary to trace the actual historical relationships between these teachings as they developed. The history of the teachings was what was important, not so much the individual teachings themselves. In his *Lectures* Baur attempted to present such a history. He distinguished three periods represented by *(a)* Paul and Revelation; *(b)* Hebrews, the shorter Letters of Paul (including Philippians but not the Pastorals), the catholic Letters (excluding those of John) and the synoptic Gospels and Acts; and *(c)* the Pastorals and John's Gospel and Letters.

Baur was already in something of a quandary with regard to the teaching of Jesus as distinct from the synoptic Gospels. As was to be the case in many a subsequent New Testament theology, he accorded it a special status. Although it represented a distinct period, it was not treated on the same level as the others. The teaching of Jesus represented the principles to which the others related merely as derived and secondary. Only the developments subsequent to Jesus, according to Baur, were the real subject matter of New Testament theology. Thus the teaching of Jesus represented not the first but the primeval period.

2. The Limits of Baur's Understanding of New Testament Theology as History

Gabler, as we noted, understood the New Testament religion very much in the sense of teachings. In a remarkable way Baur maintained a similar understanding of the New Testament history. It was a history of what was thought and taught, the beginning of the history of doctrine, not a history of what happened or was experienced or of a religion. But whereas Gabler tacitly assumed that the New Testament religion was a teaching, it became an explicit issue with which Baur was confronted by Christian Friedrich Schmid's *Biblical Theology of the New Testament*.

Schmid understood New Testament theology as the historical-genetic presentation of all aspects of New Testament *Christianity*. This included teachings, but only secondarily. In many ways Schmid was a precursor of the interpretation of New Testament theology as the history of New Testament religion. Christianity expressed itself in the New Testament as a new religion which had relationships of contrast and of continuity with pre-Christian religions, the Old Testament as well as others. This new religion was not primarily a teaching but the experiencing of a new life in God through Christ and through the Holy Spirit. Only secondarily, and as a result of that, did it become partly teaching, partly institution, especially the institution of a community.

According to Baur, Schmid's conception of New Testament theology contradicted not only the accepted meaning of the word *theology* but also the nature of the subject matter itself. In a New Testament theology one did not want to know what went on in connection with the birth of Jesus, in his ministry, and so on, and also not what the apostles did but what had been the nature of their teachings, their *Lehrbegriffe* or doctrines. Baur thus understood New Testament theology as history in a narrowly defined sense: it was not the history of what New Testament Christians experienced, or of their religion, but of the teachings developed by them.

In addition to these objections in principle to Schmid's conception of New Testament theology, Baur also mentioned the following practical difficulty. An historical-genetic presentation of New Testament Christianity in Schmid's sense could not be made solely on the basis of the material presented by the New Testament itself. The teaching contained in the New Testament, on the other hand, was rounded off in itself, making it unnecessary to appeal to sources other than the New Testament writings themselves for an understanding of it.

Baur, thus, opened new dimensions for an understanding of the New Testament as history by moving beyond what was contained in the writings themselves to the historical relationships between these writings as they developed. But his conception of New Testament theology as history was intentionally limited to the historical development of *the teachings*. In that regard his understanding was still very similar to Gabler's conception of a true biblical theology. Gabler's conception was rooted in the recognition that the Bible did not contain a theology but a religion. However, he conceived of that religion as a teaching. What needed to be recognized was that religion was not limited to a teaching, indeed, was not even primarily a teaching. When that was recognized it had to become clear that a true biblical theology could not be a theology at all but a systematic history of New Testament religion. In that regard it was comparable to neither a history of doctrine nor a history of pure philosophy.

Baur's rejection of all but teaching as irrelevant for an interpretation of New Testament theology eliminated the possibilities inherent in Gabler's conception of a true biblical theology. Baur was correct, of course, in maintaining that what Schmid described as New Testament theology could not really have been considered theology. What followed from that, however, was not that it should have been excluded from further consideration but that a history of New Testament thought was not understandable as a history of doctrine. And if it was not possible to investigate such a history on the basis of the New Testament alone, the obvious step should have been to make use of whatever other material was available. Both of these conclusions were precisely what Deissmann suggested.

3. *The New Testament Religion and Its Primitive Christian and Non-Christian Environment: Adolf Deissmann*

To begin with, Deissmann rejected Baur's contention that in writing a New Testament history one must either choose the New Testament itself as the only source or depend on other sources as well.

He believed that whether one limited oneself to the New Testament canon or freed oneself from the limits set by the canon, the results would have been the same. If one started one's investigation with a wide range of sources beyond the canonical limits, the specific value of the writings collected in the New Testament canon would very soon be recognized, and if, on the other hand, one started with the canon alone, it would in due course have become clear that the dividing line between canonical and extracanonical materials was fluid. Deissmann nevertheless chose the position which was not restricted by the limits of the canon because he believed that the historian should avoid "even the appearance" of a predetermined route of inquiry.

Obviously, for Deissmann New Testament Christianity, and thus a theology of the New Testament, was not understandable on the basis of the New Testament alone. But consideration of the New Testament within the context of primitive Christianity as a whole did not have to blind one to the particular value of the New Testament itself. This did not mean an appeal to the New Testament as divinely revealed truth but a recognition of its distinctive value similar to that of an individual of genius in history. One is reminded of his subsequent great study of *Paul: A Study in Social and Religious History*.[12]

Christianity, Deissmann pointed out, emerged on Jewish soil, but already in the earliest period it broke through the boundaries of its national identity and opened itself to the entire Hellenistic world. Thus, one could not limit the scope of the background against which Christianity became understandable only to the Old Testament. Indeed, it was not even modern historical exegesis of the Old Testament that aided in a better understanding of the New Testament. One needed to find out how the Old Testament was interpreted in the time of the New Testament. In that regard also the Old Testament Apocrypha and Pseudepigrapha, as well as Josephus and Philo, became indispensable. With regard to the non-Jewish literature, Deissmann considered as especially important later Stoic thought, less so earlier Greek philosophy. He does not appear at the time when he gave his lecture to have become aware of the importance of the Hellenistic religions, which became so decisively important for the *Religionsgeschichtliche* school. Deissmann was aware that the interpretation of the New Testament against its background was a task of such proportions that it may very well have required a sepa-

---

12. Adolf Deissmann, *Paulus: Eine kultur- und religionsgeschichtliche Skizze*, 2d ed. (Tübingen: J. C. B. Mohr [Paul Siebeck], 1925); English translation, *Paul: A Study in Social and Religious History*, trans. William E. Wilson (Gloucester, Mass.: Peter Smith, 1958).

rate discipline, such as we now have in the discipline of New Testament background, sometimes separately as Jewish and as Hellenistic background. (The latter designations are misleading because in large part Jewish thought in New Testament times would also have to be designated distinctively Hellenistic as compared with other periods of its history.)

In direct opposition to Baur, Deissmann rejected the notion that New Testament thought could be investigated in terms of a teaching or teachings. There were, of course, portions that could have been characterized as teaching, but not even in Paul could the fundamentally practical nature of such passages be denied. Nothing in Paul was ever specifically theological. What he wrote was in the first place confessional, a human mind struggling with the religious particularism of his time. Even in the more theological passages, nothing like a theological system was recognizable. In that regard Deissmann considered it a remnant of the old doctrine of verbal inspiration when it was assumed that all Paul's statements had to fit into a well-thought-through theological system. Nowhere has it been stated more clearly than here by Deissmann that Paul's thought could have been understood properly only if it was recognized as primarily religious and not theological.

A further important distinction which Deissmann made was between the systematic presentation of a history and a systematic theology. With that, in a sense, he reaffirmed Gabler's distinction between a systematic presentation of the history of biblical thought in a true biblical theology and the purified system of thought derived from it in a pure biblical theology. A similar distinction would have been possible between a systematic presentation of the history of Stoic thought and a specific system of Stoic philosophy.

According to Deissmann, the unity of the New Testament was not to be found in an intellectual system of thought but in the relationship which all the conceptions of salvation in the New Testament had to the person of Jesus. With that he once more brought into focus the difference between theology as a coherent system of thought on matters relating to the divine and a variety of different convictions which could even have been contradictory but all of which were related to a single factor. The unity in the New Testament identified by Deissmann reminds one of Luther's grounding of his thinking in what he considered the central theme of the Bible, the justification of the sinner, and his rejection of theology as a coherent system of thought. For Luther too *was Christum treibet*, what promoted Christ, was the central factor which determined the underlying unity of the Bible. It should be borne in mind, however, that for Luther it was not any relationship to Christ but a relationship defined by the doctrine of justification by faith alone. The mere relationship to Jesus, as interpreted by Deissmann, was more inclusive. As a matter of fact it included, in principle, all the "heresies" as well. The question is whether one can meaningfully speak of heresy from such a point of view. This understanding of the unity of the New Testament in terms of a relationship to Jesus, rather than of a coherent system of thought, was to find a subsequent advocate in Adolf Schlatter, in his *New Testament Theology*, and, following him, in Ernst Käsemann.

B. A PROGRAM FOR THE HISTORY OF NEW TESTAMENT THEOLOGY AND RELIGION: WILLIAM WREDE

1. *The Independence of New Testament Theology*

In William Wrede many of the lines of development up to that point came together. Drawing his own conclusions from the insights available, he produced a program for what he still called a theology of the New Testament but which was by his own description in reality a history of primitive Christian religion and theology in which theology played a very minor role compared with religion.

According to Wrede, it had been very much accepted in his time—although not consistently practiced—that in a New Testament theology the New Testament writers had to be interpreted from their own point of view and not from that of the interpreter. His program was an attempt to make this a reality. An inquiry into New Testament theology had to be free from any sense of the normativity of Scripture or of the obligation to provide moral edification for the church. A New Testament theology had to be bound by a single motivation only, namely, to understand the New Testament writings in the sense in which they had been intended by their authors and in the sense of their own time.

With regard to this conception of Wrede, we should recognize that it is, of course, not really possible to understand writings from the past in the way they had been intended by their authors because we do not share the presuppositions of that time. On the other hand, however, and in a different sense, we can understand them better because we have a more complete perspective on their time than those who had been involved in it. In one sense we can understand an author better than he understood himself or his contemporary readers understood him because we have access to the total historical framework of influences that determined him and his readers. But in another sense we cannot understand what had been written in the way they did because we do not experience these influences concretely as they did. There are advantages and disadvantages in the process of understanding both ways.

Wrede also affirmed the importance of the Jewish and non-Jewish environment of the New Testament as the context in which it became understandable. According to him, the presentation of a New Testament theology was to be preceded by a discussion of the main trends of the late Jewish religion and theology, Palestinian and Alexandrian separately. The non-Jewish environment of Christianity was not to be discussed already at that stage, but in the context of the movement of Christianity into the gentile world. It appears from Wrede's remarks that he did not understand the investigation of the environment of New Testament Christianity as part of New Testament theology itself. The presentation of the outlines of that environment in a theology of the New Testament had to be made on the basis of separate investigations.

With Wrede, thus, the point had been reached at which the attempt was made to bridge the historical distance separating the New Testament from the contemporary Christian by transposing the interpreter into the setting of New Testament times. Whereas in the Middle Ages the New Testament (indeed, the Bible as a whole) had in effect been transposed into the setting of contemporary Christianity, it was now the comtemporary interpreter who had to be transposed into the setting of the New Testament. However, with that the problem how the New Testament could have functioned as the basis and norm of comtemporary Christianity was not resolved. Indeed, Wrede intensified the difficulty by insisting that it was not the task of the investigation of the New Testament religion and theology to provide material for dogmatic theology or edification for contemporary Christianity.

Wrede's conception of a New Testament theology, thus, looks very much like an implementation of Gabler's intentions for a true biblical theology, except that Wrede did not provide for a New Testament theology in the narrower sense in which account was taken of whatever in the New Testament still had contemporary significance. With regard to New Testament theology in the broader sense, however, his intentions were very much the same as Gabler's, namely, that dogmatic theology or practical theological considerations were not to determine one's investigation of the history of New Testament religion and theology. He did indeed not reject all consideration of ways in which the New Testament could have provided edification for contemporary Christianity. According to him, however, that was not the task of a New Testament theology but of other disciplines such as exegesis or monographs on individual New Testament authors in which the relevance of the New Testament writings for such matters could have been brought out.

Although Wrede thus did not envisage a New Testament theology in the context of the comprehensive task of theological investigation, as Gabler had done, his purpose was congruent with that of Gabler, to provide for a truly historical interpretation of the New Testament religion and theology without being influenced by dogmatics or by considerations of edification. What he proposed could very well be conceived of as a more developed program for Gabler's true biblical theology but without giving attention to how it related to the rest of the task of interpretation.

2. The Break with the Canon

With Deissmann, Wrede also emphasized the necessity of breaking with the New Testament canon. According to Wrede, rejection of the doctrine of divine inspiration implied rejection of the limits of the canon. The New Testament writings themselves did not claim to be canonical (or to have been bound to each other as a canon). To subject oneself to the limits of the canon was to subject oneself to the judgment of the bishops and theologians of the first Christian centuries. The appreciation of the New Testament writings in the early church at large had also not been in terms of defined limits, such as of a canon, but of fluid lines of distinction between the relative value of the various writings of primitive Christianity.

The canon, thus, did not provide the appropriate framework for the task at hand. In the presentation of the history of primitive Christian religion and theology, everything that belonged together in terms of subject matter had to be taken together, not what had been grouped together by the accident of the canon. In a number of cases canonical writings were closer in intention to noncanonical ones than they were to others in the canon, for example, Hebrews was closer to Barnabas than to Paul, James to 1 Clement or to the Shepherd of Hermas, and John to Ignatius.

In considering a cutting-off point for such inquiry, Wrede proposed that it would have had to be where one phase of the development came to an end and a new phase started. He considered this point to have been reached with the transition to the apologists since they looked back on a development that had been relatively complete. It was a turning point, however, which itself was not without a certain fluidity and which was thus not to be taken too rigidly.

3. The Problem of the New Testament as Theology

In what appears almost a contradiction of Baur, Wrede described the purpose of New Testament theology as to know what was believed, thought, taught, hoped, demanded, and sought after in the earliest period of Christianity. The task of New Testament theology was to present with the greatest clarity possible the characteristics of primitive Christian thought and experience and to teach us to understand those historically. The task was not to determine what information certain writings contained concerning faith, doctrine, hope, and so on. In another sense, however, Wrede's program was a radical carrying out of Baur's proposal of a thoroughly historical interpretation of New Testament theology. The task was not to investigate the religious and moral *content* of the New Testament writings but the *history* of primitive Christian religion and theology.

Wrede agreed with Baur that New Testament theology was not concerned with the contents of the individual writings but with the history of New Testament Christian thought, of which these were products and on the basis of which alone they were understandable. His disagreement with Baur concerned the nature of that history. Baur understood it as a history of doctrine, but to Wrede it was very clear that the New Testament contained very little that could have been considered doctrine or teaching. A teaching, he argued, was present only when an author developed thoughts and ideas with the purpose of teaching. There was very little of that nature in the New Testament. A history of the New Testament religion and theology, thus, was not comparable with a history of doctrine or a history of philosophy where the lines of development did indeed run from teaching(s) to teaching(s), in many cases on the basis almost entirely of written materials.

By taking the New Testament in the sense of a history of teachings or of doctrine, an arbitrary evenness was imposed on it, the evenness of a single type of writing, of teaching, which meant either leaving out of consideration or misrepresenting the largest part of the New Testament material which was not teaching but, for example, narratives with religious-ethical implications, or writings of pastoral involvement and concern, and so on. All distinctions disappeared and everything became gray, being neither clearly distinguishable as teaching nor as something else. Of all New Testament writers, Paul was the only one who did reflect on matters in the way of a theologian, but even in his case it would have been an imposition of severe limits on the interpretation to have taken him as a theologian. Even his doctrine of justification by faith was rooted in the practical concern for the gentile mission.

4. The Distinction of Levels of Meaning

Related to the interpretation of the New Testament almost entirely in the sense of teachings, of theology, was the tendency of taking every detail in it as of equal importance. Every statement, every term even, was assumed to have been of equal importance as an expression of a theology, to the degree even of almost taking each statement or term as expressing by itself an entire theology. This tendency is still present today in word studies and in contemporary commentaries in which almost every verse, construction, or word is discussed on an equal level with every other. There was validity, according to Wrede, in the charge that New Testament theology was the discipline of minutiae and of insignificant nuances.

The method of defining the meanings of words with final definiteness was based on the assumption that New Testament writers worked with similar systematic precision. So, for example, he argued that *flesh* in Paul should not be taken as a precisely defined systematic concept but as a term that varied in meaning as it was used to give expression to more fundamental matters such as sin, righteousness, the Law, death, this age, the spirit, and so on. The term for Paul did not have a clearly defined meaning. As examples Wrede could have given many other terms which continue to baffle New Testament scholars because they do not fit into a pattern of consistent systematic usage. For example, *law* could refer to the Torah but also to a principle, for example, of works or of grace (Rom. 3:7), or to the law which the Gentiles fulfill "by nature" (Rom. 2:14). *Justification* was understood, on the one hand, to have been by faith in Christ alone (Rom. 3:21, etc.) but also to have been based on what the Law required (Rom. 2:13). In the attempts to define such terms with precision in the sense of systematic thought, essential meanings were frequently missed or remained indistinguishable from what was circumstantial with regard to the level of their significance.

With these observations Wrede not only distinguished between the systematic, clearly defined usage of terms and the more usual way in which ordinary language functions. He also anticipated some of the more recent insights of linguistics that meaning in ordinary language usage cannot be clarified by means of the definition of individual terms but by the recognition of their functions in areas of meanings (semantic domains) that are codetermined by a number of words in relationship to each other. Individual words only seemingly have defined meanings. Their real meanings are as functions, within a semantic domain, and thus are constantly codetermined by their relationships to other words in such a domain. So, for instance, Paul uses the term *flesh* in relationship to all the other terms referred to by Wrede, as mentioned above. This is true even of systematic thought, where the functions are merely defined more consistently and precisely within the domain of an entire system of thought than is the case with ordinary language usage.

5. The Problem of the Literary Level of New Testament Thought

Related to these was another complaint of Wrede against New Testament theology, namely, that it proceeded on the assumption that everything took place at the level of literature, as if it was possible to determine what was taking place in the history of primitive Christian thought by taking only written documents into consideration, as if there had been direct connections between the various New Testament writings. In reality, according to him, the thought connections tended to be largely indirect as a result of their being expressions of a common developing religious and cultural heritage. Even where direct literary dependence did exist, there was not necessarily an interrelatedness of meaning. For example, the meaning of material taken over by another author from Paul may have been determined more by that author's own context than by what Paul had intended. Wrede's point can be illustrated very clearly by reference to the interrelatedness of the tradition in the synoptic Gospels. The meanings of that tradition shifted constantly during the period of oral transmission, as well as when the Synoptics quoted it from each other.

The primitive Christian writings were products of a living religion, not theological reflections on a literary level. Thus the fine distinctions between authors, as if they were involved in precise theological controversy with each other, and even between statements of an individual author had to be given up for the sake of discovering the lines of development which were, as living experience, at the basis of what was thought. In a living religion almost every important change was determined by religious-historical processes, very little by the reading of literature. Thus what may have appeared as highly significant differences in terms of developed systematic thinking may have been merely alternate expressions of the same factors in a living religion, whether of more than one or of a single author.

In the then current New Testament theology, however, Wrede

found the New Testament treated as a series of individual teachings, as a summary of what was taught by a number of relatively minor theologians, related to each other at the most in a chronological sequence with only occasional back references. There was almost no sensitivity to the much more powerful developing religion on which their teachings were based. These theologies usually gave the impression that the primitive Christian conceptions were pure products of the mind, as if they were developed in a world of their own hovering above the course of ordinary history.

6. *The New Testament a Product of a Living Religion*

In all of this the central issue may have been the tendency—which still exists today—to discuss everything in theNew Testament at the same level of importance, as if every detail was decisive. Detailed study, according to Wrede, was necessary where it was called for, but not indiscriminate attention to everything available. That did not imply ignoring the significance of individuals or of individual expressions. To the contrary, precisely by recognizing contributions within the framework of the general development, it became possible to appreciate the significance of individual expressions and the contributions of individual writers in proper perspective. Not the individual views as such were important but the relevance which they had within the larger picture.

This did not apply only to the more important writings. In the case of minor writings many details were so insignificant in themselves as to have made their individual discussion ridiculous. As part of a general development, however, such details could have been highly significant. So, for example, the conception of the death of Christ, of the church as the true Israel, or of the alienation of Christians on earth in 1 Peter were insignificant when taken by themselves but not when recognized in terms of their fruitfulness in helping to clarify historical developments in primitive Christianity. On the other hand, what may have been purely circumstantial was frequently elevated to the distinction of an important concept, for example, when 1 Peter was interpreted as "the apostle of hope" merely because the term *hope* occurred frequently in this Letter. In reality the frequent occurrence of the term may have been due almost entirely to the particular circumstances in which the author of 1 Peter wrote. Almost anybody else who wrote in the same situation would probably have used the term with similar frequency. Its usage, thus, was probably purely circumstantial and may not have revealed anything in particular about the author. Another example was where the very dearth of information led an interpreter to attach exaggerated importance to the little that could be found, for example, the discussion of "election" in James even though the Letter of James contained only two very general references to the concept.

A mere chronological sequence of writings provided only a very rough indication of the development. What was necessary was to try to uncover the development behind such writings as that to which they gave expression. Such a procedure would not have been possible if the inquiry was limited only to teachings because that would have left out the most important aspects of the development. It had still been possible for Baur to present such a development purely in terms of teachings because he proceeded on the basis of a preconceived scheme of history into which he fitted the teachings. The problem was merely whether the scheme provided by Baur was that in terms of which the New Testament history actually took place. What was necessary was that every meaningful conception, every idea that became effective, every important outlook had to be recognized as a living product of a religious history according to the same laws which determined the growth of conceptions, ideas, and outlooks at any other time.

7. Toward a History of New Testament Religion and Theology

In such a history, according to Wrede, the views of a single author would have required individual mention only if his thoughts had great influence on the development, or if he at least had a distinctive conception of faith, or maybe even if his writing revealed only at least some individual, clearly recognizable features. On this basis Wrede concluded that the only individuals and writings worthy of particular discussion were Jesus, Paul, John, and Ignatius.

A second group of writings, Revelation, Hebrews, and Barnabas, did not call for separate discussion because none of them was responsible for a distinct, comprehensive religious conception. Although they may have provided a few individual formulations here and there, on the whole they represented ideas, moods, or interests that were very general in nature. Their significance was in providing material by means of which it became possible to recognize some of the important features of primitive Christianity, as well as to interpret its development.

A third group, 1 Peter, the Synoptics and Acts (that is, as individual writings rather than as reproducing decisively important traditions), 1 Clement, James, the Didache, the Pastorals, 2 Peter, Jude, Polycarp, and the Shepherd of Hermas, did not represent a single view with such special clarity or in such a way that one could say that through them an idea became normative or gained recognition or was created by them. These writings represented ordinary Christianity. Only Jesus, Paul, John, and Ignatius, thus, deserved separate treatment. Consequently, they determined the shape of Wrede's proposed New Testament theology. A history of primitive Christian religion and theology would have been distorted if it did not recognize the individual significance of, respectively, Jesus, Paul, John, and Ignatius. Similarly, it would have been a distortion to make more of the second group, Revelation, Hebrews, and Barnabas, than as sources for uncovering the more general developments they represented.

According to Wrede, it was even more important than in connection with the individual figures or writers that particular conceptions, for example, primitive Christian eschatology, were not to be discussed in terms of individual views but of the general flow of thought. It was the general flow that was really influential most of the time, only rarely the contributions of individuals. Thus, giving attention to the general flow of thought did not have to mean ignoring the influence of individuals where this did occur. However, giving specific attention to the views of every minor, uninfluential writer could only have distorted what had been really taking place. Indeed, only by remaining sensitive to the general development would it have been possible to appreciate the particular contributions of both major and of minor figures. Even conceptions such as allegory in Hebrews or poverty and beneficence in Luke could have been evaluated properly only when they were considered within the larger frame of reference of the more general development. The same was true for highly individual contributions such as Paul's conception of justification by faith alone, which could also have been evaluated properly only within the general framework of the developments within which Paul had found it necessary to argue the point.

Furthermore, Wrede observed—what is today taken for granted—that with regard to their own contributions the Synoptic evangelists should not be discussed in the beginning of a New Testament theology, together with Jesus' teaching, but much later, even after Paul. On the other hand, he pointed to the distortion which occurred when the entire development between Paul and John was interpreted as having been under Paul's influence and when the Johannine view was interpreted one-sidedly as the culmination of that development. The history of New Testament Christianity had been much more complicated.

8. Wrede's Outline for a Theology of the New Testament

Briefly, then, Wrede suggested the following outline for a New Testament theology:

(a) Jesus. The teaching which we have of him was not separable from the significance of his person and the recognizable events of his life. It should be noted, thus, that Wrede was not concerned with the "historical" Jesus but with Jesus as he became effective in the development of New Testament religion and theology, that is, not with Jesus as an individual but as the one who was decisively important for the origin and development of the Christian faith.

(b) The primitive church. There was very little information concerning it. The chapter, thus, would have been rather brief.

(c) Paul. Only specifically Pauline features should come into consideration; others, insofar as they represent Christianity at large, belong to the discussion of the church of his time.

(d) Gentile Christianity. Here conceptions such as the attitude toward Judaism, ethics as a general Christian concern, and so on should be discussed.

(e) John.

(f) Ignatius. Wrede seemed to be, after all, rather cautious about devoting a completely separate chapter to him. He suggested that it may be best to discuss him in relationship to John where he most naturally belonged.

9. The Problem of the Name "Theology of the New Testament"

The most disappointing aspect of Wrede's program was that he did not take the problem of the designation seriously. He stated very explicitly that what was involved in the study was a primitive Christian history of religion, or the history of primitive Christian religion and theology, but then added that it would have been remarkable if one did not consider the designation "New Testament theology" as appropriate for such a study. The name, he argued, obviously adapted itself to the subject matter and not the other way around. By refusing to concede that in fact he did not propose a "theology" of the New Testament in the proper sense, Wrede failed to recognize that there still remained a distinctive task which could more appropriately have been designated as "New Testament theology," that is, the task, more or less, which Gabler attributed to a pure theology of the New Testament.

10. The Problem of a "Theology" of Paul

Less than a decade later, Wrede published a small volume on Paul (*Paulus,* 1905, and a second edition already in 1907, the year after his death at only forty-seven). It comprised four chapters, on Paul's "personality," his "lifework," his "theology," and "the place of Paul in the history of the emerging Christianity." Of the 106 pages, 43, that is, about forty percent, were devoted to Paul's theology, indicating its relative importance. This is in agreement with Wrede's understanding expressed in the programmatic essay that of all New Testament writers Paul most clearly reflected on matters in the way of a theologian. Nevertheless, Wrede pointed out, one could not think in terms of modern concepts when one called Paul a theologian. Not even in Romans did he attempt to develop his teaching into a theological system. He always wrote as a missionary, as an organizer, and as a public speaker, developing his thoughts ad hoc for each particular situation and in every case taking up only one side of an argument, never systematically considering every possibility.

Thus, Wrede wondered again whether *theology* was the correct term to use in connection with Paul but concluded that it was unavoidable. In the first place, there was a firm theological element in Paul's way of thinking, especially when he became polemical. What Wrede had in mind was Paul's rabbinic type of reasoning and the way he appealed to Scripture in support of an argument. Secondly, Paul valued "knowledge" in the sense that he did not merely preach the gospel to mature Christians but communicated to them what he called wisdom, even though it was not human wisdom but a type of "science of the inspired."

According to Wrede, Paul did develop a comprehensive outlook, comprising many theological presuppositions, assertions, and conclusions. Thus, to a certain degree, he presented Christianity as a construction of thought. Consequently, it was as wrong to think that one could describe Paul's piety without taking into consideration the thoughts with which he grasped the meaning of Christ and of his death and resurrection as it was to think of him in terms of a rational teaching that was beyond all piety and could have been grasped by means of the mind alone. Paul's religion was theological; his theology was religion. On the other hand, although Paul's thinking did have firmly established main lines, it moved very lightly from Letter to Letter and from chapter to chapter without a concern for logical consistency in the details. It was very easy to recognize numerous contradictions in the Pauline letters.

WHAT IS NEW TESTAMENT THEOLOGY?

Paul was the first Christian theologian, the creator of a Christian theology. He took the first step from religion to theology, a step of fundamental significance, according to Wrede. At first sight it seemed like a stepping down from what was simple, immediate, alive to something complex, mediated, a product of reflection. But subsequently one recognized that it was a necessity, that it was the condition for the preservation and continued effectiveness of a religion.

These reflections reveal how difficult it was to distinguish between religion and theology. Concretely, the question was in this case whether Paul's thinking was primarily religious or theological. The difficulty is particularly evident when Wrede discussed what Paul did as a theologian, namely, that he transformed Christianity into a religion of redemption. Paul's greatest innovation was the way in which he made the events of salvation, that is, the becoming human, death, and resurrection of Christ, into the foundations of the Christian religion, for example, in the Philippians hymn. According to Wrede, the term *myth* becomes unavoidable for describing Paul's method in this case. In discussing Paul as a theologian, thus, Wrede advanced from understanding him as a theological thinker to an understanding of him as a creator of a *religion* by means of the telling of a *myth*. It almost seems as if we have come back to the original meaning of the term *theology* as it had been used by Plato: the composition of a myth. Undoubtedly that was not Wrede's intent, but it is obvious that, unlike Gabler, he did not have a clearly defined conception of theology. At the same time these observations, especially as they relate to Paul, who so obviously stood on the borderline between religion and theology, are very revealing as far as the problem of a theology of New Testament is concerned.

11. The Achievements and Limits of Wrede's Program

Probably the greatest achievement of Wrede was that he brought into clear view the New Testament religion and theology as an entity in its own right and not merely as a framework or backdrop for a contemporary Christianity. In contrast with the Middle Ages, when the Bible was taken to be contemporary with medieval Christianity, Wrede's program demanded that the present-day interpreter be transposed to the times of the New Testament. Correspondingly, he also demanded that the New Testament be understood in its own terms, primarily as the reflection of a developing religion and not as a theology in the modern sense. The New Testament writings did not constitute a history of teachings, of doctrines, or of theology which took place at a literary level. They were the product of a living religion of which only a small part had come down in writing. One might compare the history of the New Testament religion with the flow of a river, and the New Testament writings with ripples caused by the flow of the water. The task, thus, was as much as possible to attend to the history of that religion on the basis of the available materials.

However, letting oneself in on the New Testament as the reflection of the New Testament religion and theology in its own right did not only mean to surrender contemporary theological assumptions. It also meant a disregard for the theological and church-political activities of the first Christian centuries which led to the establishment of a canon. In and of itself, there could be no objection to limiting research to a canon as far as the church of the first centuries was concerned and also of the centuries that followed. However, regarding the New Testament writings themselves, the canon indeed imposed an artificial context on them, quite contrary to the way in which they were understood by both their authors and their first readers. For that reason, the limits of the canon had to be given up when interpreting the New Testament. All the available material, canonical and noncanonical, that could contribute to an understanding of New Testament Christianity had to be taken into consideration. This included the non-Christian environment of primitive Christianity as well, Jewish and non-Jewish, as the real context within which Christianity could become understandable.

Wrede also reaffirmed that the New Testament did not contain a theology, or at least not more than a bare minimum of theology. In doing so he rejected the arbitrary evenness which had been imposed on the New Testament by interpreting it as a theology. The New Testament writings contained a variety of types of expression, for example, pastoral concern, preaching, narrative, and so on, all of which were expressions of a living religion. Various levels of significance of both the individual writings as well as the conceptions in them needed to be recognized. Interpreted within the context of primitive Christianity as a living religion, the New Testament writings could have become more fully understandable.

Great as his contribution was, however, there are two areas where it is necessary to go beyond him: in the areas of the non-Christian environment of primitive Christianity and of the meaning of theology. In the case of the former, it is simply a question of carrying further the suggestions of his program, but with regard to the latter, his conception of theology must be considered as still very ill defined.

Wrede's program did not provide for the history of the New Testament religion to be interpreted as an integral part of the large movement of Hellenistic religious experience and thought. The other religions were still only the background of primitive Christianity. Although the limits of the New Testament canon had been broken, his program still remained very much within the limits of the Christian movement. A widening of the context within which primitive Christianity was interpreted would have enhanced the possibility of understanding the New Testament writings because it would then have become a matter of merely interpreting the available details within this larger framework instead of having to reconstruct the history of primitive Christianity from the sparse details provided by the New Testament and other primitive Christian literature.

That larger context was already being uncovered in Wrede's time by the *Religionsgeschichtliche* school, of which he was a member. The fundamental characteristic of that school had been to interpret primitive Christianity consistently within the framework of the religions of the time. Other major members of the school were Albert Eichhorn (1856–1926), Hermann Gunkel (1862–1932), Bousset, Johannes Weiss (1863–1914), and Wilhelm Heitmuller (1869–1926). A contributor from the area of philology was Richard Reitzenstein (1861–1931). Moreover, the school was able to draw heavily also from the work of other philologist-interpreters of religion such as Franz Cumont (1868–1947), Eduard Norden (1868–1941), and Albrecht Dieterich (1866–1908); for Stoicism on Max Pohlenz (1872–1962); and for the area of Jewish thought on Paul Volz (1871–1941) and Gustav Dalman (1855–1941).

An example of how such a widening of the horizon could be helpful in interpreting the New Testament is Reitzenstein's *The Hellenistic Mystery Religions* (1910). It is not an interpretation of Paul but, as the title indicates, a presentation of Hellenistic religious thought and of the general atmosphere in which they existed. Nevertheless, what it presents is also so true of the historical setting of Paul's thinking that one would not find a commentary or monograph on Paul that is more revealing of his thought. Many individual features of Paul's thought would remain incomprehensible unless understood against the background of the material presented by Reitzenstein.

As we have seen, Wrede was already pointing to all of this with his insistence that the New Testament writings be interpreted not as products of a development that took place at the level of literature or of theology but as expressions of a living religion. In doing so he outlined the program for a theology of the New Testament in accordance with the principles of the *Religionsgeschichtliche* school. And although he did not suggest the non-Christian religious environment of the New Testament as very much more than the *background* of the primitive Christian religion, the fundamental principles of his program were in agreement with Bousset's interpretation of the history of the New Testament religion as an integral part of the general religious development of the Hellenistic age. To have understood primitive Christianity as an integral part of the general history of the Hellenistic age did not imply having to ignore its individuality, as little as it meant having to ignore the individual contributions of New Testament writers or writings when they were interpreted as integral parts of the developing New Testament religion. Indeed, only now was it possible to recognize what had been truly individual.

The purely historical interpretation of the New Testament as a product of a living religion required great clarity concerning its relationship to a theological interpretation and concerning the difference between the two types of interpretation. By not distinguishing his program for a history of primitive Christian religion and theology from a theology of the New Testament, Wrede failed to recognize the possibility of the latter as an independent discipline, as Gabler had done with his distinction between a true and a pure biblical theology. Unlike in the practice of the Christian religion in the church, the academic study of religion had to contend for a theological interpretation of the Bible or the New Testament because its meaning was not taken for granted. The New Testament is not the subject of academic interest in its own right. One is interested in the New Testament because it is part of the Scriptures of a believing religious community. The question thus arises unavoidably as to what the New Testament means. But even where the New Testament writings could be of interest apart from their being part of the Christian Scriptures, the question of what they mean remains unavoidable. If there were to be no expectation that these writings had something meaningful to say, there would be very little interest in them.

By not providing for a separate New Testament theology, Wrede failed to ensure that theological interests would not once more invade the historical study of the New Testament religion and theology. The thin edge of the wedge may have been the inclusion of *theology* in the designation. It was in connection with Paul, as we have seen, that the problematic nature of that designation became clear: is *theology* the correct term for Paul's thinking? Especially revealing is Wrede's remark that Paul's religion was theological and that his theology was religion. Given this premise, it must be considered misleading for Wrede to have written of the New Testament religion *and* theology since Paul's theology was in fact also religion. And Paul was the only one whose thinking even approached being theological.

In discussing Paul as a theologian, Wrede finally came to the point of interpreting his theology in the original sense of the term, that is, as the production of a myth. That is obviously a valid usage of the term, but misleading. As Wrede himself recognized, it did not refer to anything that was called a theology in his (Wrede's) time. That the term *theology* was used to refer to a number of phenomena did not make a single phenomenon of them. Even though Paul may have had a theology in the original sense of the term, that did not make a presentation of his thought a "theology of Paul" in the modern, more precise sense of the term. Such a presentation could have been, at the most, a systematic presentation of his thought in an historical sense.

In order for the meaning of the New Testament writings in a contemporary sense to be clarified, whether it be for the Christian religious community or because of general interest in the humanities, a separate discipline was required. That leaves either Gabler's distinction between two types of the biblical (or New Testament) theology or, if we follow the more thorough approach of Wrede in his program, the distinction between a historical presentation of the developing primitive Christian religion and a theology of the New Testament. In both cases the latter still had to be distinguished from a dogmatic theology, developing a coherent, logical, necessary system of general ideas in terms of which every element of our experience concerning matters relating to God is interpreted. That such a dogmatic theology could, by choice or by conviction, be based on a New Testament or a biblical theology, as Gabler had intended, remains, of course, always a possibility.

On the other hand, it has become clear that a New Testament theology could not be as "pure" in the sense of eternal divine truths as Gabler had hoped. The most that could be achieved was to lift out of the New Testament what was still meaningful today. This task has not yet been taken up systematically.

C. THE HISTORY OF PRIMITIVE CHRISTIAN RELIGION: WILHELM BOUSSET

1. Bousset's Relationship to the Program of Wrede

Wilhelm Bousset did not specifically carry out Wrede's program as such. Nevertheless, his *Kyrios Christos* (1913) was in effect the carrying out of its fundamental intentions. Of course, Wrede's program was not particularly his own but the articulation of views characteristic of the *Religionsgeschichtliche* school of which he and Bousset were both members. Bousset gave the following very apt description of the purpose of Wrede's programmatic essay: It was an action against a type of research that was characterized by excessive fussiness, a purposeless busyness, wanting to know everything, suffering from the curse of having to be at all costs complete. In contrast, Wrede argued for a broader style and for a vigorous search for what was essential. Especially the latter characterized also Bousset's *Kyrios Christos*. As "a history of the belief in Christ from the beginnings of Christianity to Irenaeus," it qualifies very well as an implementation of the intentions of Wrede's program.

True, with regard to details, Bousset deviated from Wrede's program in two major respects. In the first place, he did not provide a comprehensive presentation of the development of the primitive Christian religion but a presentation on the basis of a central theme, namely, of the cult of Jesus as Christ the Lord. Actually, Bousset had thought of a more comprehensive work on the development of Christianity within the framework of the Hellenistic-Roman culture, but he had become increasingly aware that the status of research in general on the subject, and particularly the limits of his own knowledge, did not permit him to undertake such a task. Nevertheless, he expressed the hope that since the history and development of the faith in Christ were so much at the center of the general development of primitive Christianity, he may at least have approximated that other, more comprehensive goal to some degree with *Kyrios Christos*.

Bousset also deviated from Wrede's program in that he did not set the end point of his study just before the apologists but continued on to Irenaeus because he considered the development of the doctrine of Christ relatively complete with Irenaeus. After Irenaeus came mere elaboration, that is, the working out of the further consequences of the development up to that stage. All the lines of development came together in Irenaeus, culminating in his answer to the question why God in Christ became man, namely, to let mankind become divine, a conception that had already been anticipated by John.

In many respects the more limited goal which Bousset had set for himself was congruent with that which he appreciated about Wrede, namely, not to suffer from the curse of having to be comprehensive at all costs but to be engaged in a vigorous search for what was essential. The limitation of the study, the focus on the cult of Christ the Lord, gave it its strength. At the same time, however, (as happens of necessity with a narrow focus) it did distort by allowing other, more than circumstantial aspects to recede into the background. Nevertheless, even though what Bousset presented was not all there was to the development of primitive Christianity, it opened a perspective to that development unequalled before and unparalleled subsequently. Whatever corrections may be needed with regard to details, *Kyrios Christos* leaves no doubt that the only access to primitive Christianity was to recognize it as having been fundamentally a religion and only secondarily, as a relatively late development, a theology.

2. The History of the Primitive Christian Religion

Although all of primitive Christianity, including the life and preaching of Jesus, as presented by Bousset, was religion, probably the most decisive characteristic of his interpretation was the exclusion of Jesus himself, or even of Palestinian Christianity, from the involvement in the cult of Christ the Lord. That cult represented a development which took place—which could only have taken place—on non-Jewish soil. It is very important to note that he was persuaded about this not on the basis of any particular argument but because of a sensitivity to the various religious mentalities of the time. It was simply inconceivable to him that Jesus could have been accorded divine worship in a Palestinian Jewish (Christian) religious community.

Probably nothing revealed more clearly the difference between the approach of the *Religionsgeschichtliche* school to the interpretation of New Testament Christianity (for whom the general developments were fundamental and the details had to fit into a general scheme) and the approach of those who tried to develop entire theories on the basis of what was considered decisive but detailed evidence. Bousset's critics appealed in particular to the Aramaic cultic formula *maranatha* (cf. 1 Cor. 16:22) as proof that Jesus had already been addressed cultically as Lord in the Palestinian Jewish Christian community. It became known as the Achilles' heel of Bousset's theory.[13] He was severely criticized for trying to explain the formula in more than one way in his writings, revealing a fundamental uncertainty about it. In *Kyrios Christos* he argued that *maranatha* did not originate in Palestine but in the bilingual region of Antioch, but in *Jesus the Lord* (1916)[14] he explained it as having

---

13. Cf. A. E. J. Rawlinson, *The New Testament Doctrine of Christ* (New York: Longmans Green & Co., 1926), pp. 231–37.

14. Wilhelm Bousset, *Jesus der Herr: Nachträge und Auseinandersetzungen zu Kyrios Christos* (Göttingen: Vandenhoeck & Ruprecht, 1916).

referred not to Jesus but to God. In the subsequent editions of *Kyrios Christos*, however, he held on to the earlier explanation.

Maranatha did provide serious difficulties for Bousset's understanding, and he knew that there had to be some explanation for its existence. He nevertheless had no doubt that the phenomenon of a cult of Jesus as Christ the Lord was inconceivable in a Palestinian Jewish religious community. He never succeeded in finding a convincing explanation for this piece of detail. Since Bousset's death, however, Siegfried Schulz[15] has shown on the basis of previously unexamined documents that *mara* in Aramaic did not have the same meaning as *kyrios* in Greek, although the terms are commonly taken as equivalents and both are translated as "Lord." *Mara* was used primarily for human authorities and only rarely and very uncommonly in reference to God in his authority as a judge. More important, whereas *kyrios* with its divine connotations was used in Hellenistic Judaism in the place of the divine name in the public reading of the Scriptures, Aramaic speaking Jews continued to use the Hebrew *adonai* rather than the Aramaic *mara*. It is not the place to discuss such details here. What is important is the approach of the *Religionsgeschichtliche* school to the interpretation of details. For them the details had to fit into the structure of larger developments which had to be discovered behind the details by making use of all the information available. It was not possible to reconstruct the development by a mere fitting together of the details. Details, such as the *maranatha* formula, were not hard facts but information that was itself in need of interpretation.

Thus, as Bousset presented it, there had been a fundamental difference between the religion of Jesus and of Palestinian Jewish Christianity, on the one hand, and the religion of Hellenistic Christianity which was characterized by the cult of Christ the Lord, on the other. That the dividing line between Palestinian and Hellenistic was not as neat as Bousset had conceived of it is not of fundamental importance here. According to him, although the Palestinian Christians embellished the image of their master, they nevertheless preserved a good part of his life that was genuine. They made him effective as a living, present symbol, preserving at the same time the simplicity of his own religion and preaching. All of that changed when Christianity in its Hellenistic setting became a cult of Christ the Lord.

Many details of Bousset's interpretation have required revision as

15. Siegfried Schulz, "Maranatha und Kyrios Christos," *Zeitschrift für die neutestamentlichen Wissenschaft* 53(1962): 125–44.

research advanced. Even some of the broader lines of development as proposed by him could not be maintained. That does not have to concern us here. What is important is that his approach remains fundamentally unaffected. A history of the primitive Christian religion, a theology of the New Testament in the broader sense of Gabler, could be investigated only in the way in which Bousset had done, that is, by trying to discover the lines of development behind the available documents. Thus he emphasized the importance of recognizing the existence of a Hellenistic Christian community before Paul, without which Paul himself would have remained incomprehensible. Paul was not understandable as a product of Palestinian Christianity. Furthermore, Bousset found it necessary to include a chapter on Gnosticism because without an understanding of the undercurrents of that movement, neither Paul, nor John, nor many of the developments that followed after them would have been comprehensible.

3. The Exclusion of Jesus from the Investigation

In a remarkable way Bousset excluded Jesus from such a submersion under the influence of the religious movements of his time. Johannes Weiss some twenty years earlier in *The Preaching of Jesus concerning the Kingdom of God* (1892) had come to the conclusion that the kingdom of God in the preaching of Jesus could not be interpreted in terms of nineteenth century conceptions. As all other New Testament concepts, it too had to be interpreted in terms of the conceptions of New Testament times, particularly in terms of Jewish apocalypticism—a view subsequently popularized by Albert Schweitzer.[16] Bousset protested that such an interpretation would have left Jesus incomprehensible. The religion of Jesus was related to Judaism in form alone. Thus, also in *Kyrios Christos*, after he had been compelled to concede that even in the case of Jesus nothing may have been completely new, he still maintained a certain particularity for Jesus in the sense of the clarity and the wholeness with which the eternal and the universally true was made to shine forth anew through him, as well as the compelling power and passion with which it took hold of the heart. With regard to Jesus, Bousset was still very much part of nineteenth-century liberalism for which the meaning of the New Testament consisted of the simple ethical religion of Jesus.

16. Albert Schweitzer, *Von Reimarus zu Wrede* (Tübingen: J. C. B. Mohr [Paul Siebeck], 1906), 2d and subsequent eds. *Geschichte der Leben-Jesu-Forschung*, 1913ff., now as Siebenstern Taschenbuch 77/78, with an intro. by James M. Robinson, München/Hamburg: Siebenstern Taschenbuch Verlag 1966; English translation, *The Quest of the Historical Jesus*, trans. W. Montgomery (London: A. and C. Black, 1910); now as a Macmillan Paperback (New York: Macmillan Co., 1962); since the 1968 ed., with an intro. by James M. Robinson.

In connection with Jesus, thus, Bousset gave up the conception of a consistent interpretation of the New Testament within the framework of the religions of the time. Jesus was interpreted on the assumption that he represented something so immediately meaningful that a prior historical interpretation in terms of the religious thinking of his own time appeared superfluous. In terms of Gabler's distinction between a biblical theology in a broader and in a narrower sense, it is almost as if the former was represented by the religious developments in the primitive church, whereas a biblical theology in the narrower, pure sense was represented by the religion and ethical teachings of Jesus. The two were related, however, not as two steps in a single, comprehensive theological task but as a distinction between two separate "theologies." But there is nothing in that approach that can demonstrate why the religion of Jesus should be exempt from the same demand of an interpretation within the framework of the religions of his own time. In that regard Johannes Weiss was more consistent.

On the other hand, it may have been precisely the exclusion of Jesus from more than a formal involvement in the religions of the time which made it possible for Bousset to pursue his investigation of the history of the cult of Christ the Lord with such consistency and thoroughness because that exclusion freed him from the restraint of being afraid to undermine his own convictions regarding the religion and ethical teachings of Jesus. *Kyrios Christos*, in any case, remains such a valuable contribution to our understanding of primitive Christian religion that this limitation was a price worth paying, especially since the process of a consistent interpretation of the teaching of Jesus within the framework of the religion of his time had already been provided by Johannes Weiss. With *Kyrios Christos*, supplemented by Weiss's *The Preaching of Jesus concerning the Kingdom of God*, the task of a historical interpretation of the New Testament religion, the task of Gabler's biblical theology of the New Testament in the broader sense, was, in a preliminary sense, complete.

SUMMARY

It was in the period covered in the present chapter that the implications of Gabler's program for a biblical theology in the broader sense, for a true biblical theology of the New Testament, were worked out in full. The end result was the realization that a true biblical theology was not a theology at all but a history of the developing primitive Christian religion.

Baur set in motion the move to a thoroughly historical interpretation of the New Testament, and Deissmann made very clear that the New Testament history was a history of a living religion, not a history of doctrines, but it was in the *Religionsgeschichtliche* school that the full implications of a thoroughly historical presentation of New Testament Christianity were realized. The outcome, however, was that the presentation of such a history became separated not only from the New Testament canon but also from usefulness for contemporary Christianity. Bousset still tried to keep Jesus out of the framework of a thoroughly historical interpretation of the New Testament Christianity within its environment, but Weiss left no doubt that Jesus too had been an integral part of that environment.

The programs of Wrede and Bousset reveal that a true biblical theology was less complicated and, therefore, in many ways easier to produce. At the same time, however, it also makes clear that it was really the mediating task of a pure biblical theology that was the most urgent. The separation of a true biblical theology of the New Testament in the sense of a history of the primitive Christian religion from usefulness for contemporary Christianity could never have lasted, because it was the demands of contemporary Christianity which continued to motivate the presentation of such a history. Two ways were proposed out of this rather incongruous situation: Schlatter rejected the very notion of a neutral presentation of the primitive Christian religion and proposed instead an interpretation of the New Testament in which historical presentation and questions of contemporary meaning were dialectically interrelated. Bultmann, on the other hand, coordinated a thoroughly historical presentation with a theological interpretation. In the case of Schlatter, historical interpretation and theological interpretation inevitably became once more intertwined, making the task of a distinct pure biblical theology of the New Testament unnecessary, but in Bultmann's program Gabler's distinction between a true and a pure biblical theology was once more reaffirmed.

IV
Theology of the
New Testament

1. The Return to a Theological Interpretation of the New Testament

In his otherwise very appreciative introductory remarks to the fifth edition of Bousset's *Kyrios Christos*, Rudolf Bultmann nevertheless expressed his regret that certain essential motifs, particularly the theology of Paul, had not received adequate attention. He conceded that Bousset in fact had not intended to write a *theology* of the New Testament but suggested that it may have become necessary now to return to the earlier question of such a theology, without surrendering, however, the insights of the *Religionsgeschichtliche* school, that is, that the New Testament could not be approached in terms of teachings or doctrines. What Bultmann was asking for was a *theology* of the New Testament that did not return to the earlier "teachings" approach and that took the work of the *Religionsgeschichtliche* school seriously as an initial step in the right direction. What was now called for was a theology of the New Testament in which "theology" was not taken in the sense of teachings or doctrines but in a sense that was more appropriate to the subject matter of the New Testament.

When Bultmann wrote this his own *Theology of the New Testament,* originally published between 1949 and 1953 in three parts, had already been established as a very significant milestone in New Testament scholarship. The concern expressed by him, however, had already been taken up four years prior to the publication of *Kyrios Christos,* by Adolf Schlatter (1852–1938) in *The Theology of the New Testament and Dogmatics* (1909) in which he outlined the principles for his *Theology of the New Testament* (vol. 1, 1909; vol. 2, 1910).

Schlatter was aware that the New Testament did not contain a theology in the strict sense of the term, but he was also convinced that the New Testament contained more than only religion. But it was not necessary to take theology in the stricter sense. After all, the church never used theology in the sense of a coherent system of timeless concepts abstracted from the concrete purposes of life. The New Testament proclamation, in any case, did not permit the separation of the act of thought from those other functions of life which together constituted our full existence. This was so not because the New Testament was still situated on a lower stage of cultural development but because it rejected as abnormal a consciousness of God that never moved beyond pure consciousness and was the basis of mere thought alone. For the New Testament, theology and ethics were inseparable. The New Testament perceived humans as completely motivated by their relationship to God, and that relationship provided the assurance which enabled them to believe in him, to serve him, and to live through him and for him. The New Testament stood in a conscious, irreconcilable contradiction to every form of thinking which produced only ideas. A New Testament theology, thus, which molded the New Testament writers in the image of Greek thinkers radically distorted its material. Schlatter produced his *Theology of the New Testament* in full awareness that it was not a theology in the strict sense of a coherent, logical, necessary system of ideas concerning God but a theology which was integral to the life of faith. Theology in the stricter sense, he argued, should be recognized as a more specialized form, as scientific *(wissenschaftliche)* theology.

2. Historical Investigation and Theological Interpretation

Like his contemporaries, Schlatter considered New Testament theology as an historical discipline. In the New Testament, theology and history were intimately related. He rejected as pre-Christian the view that history and divine revelation were contraries. God's revelation in history, in the history of Jesus, was what was characteristic of the New Testament. The theology of the New Testament, thus, did not present abstract ideas but was based on that history and remained bound to it. Nevertheless, even though New Testament history and theology were not to be separated from each other, they had to be distinguished because history as such also had a natural side, presumably such as had been investigated by the *Religionsge-*

schichtliche school. Yet only the teachings were of enduring significance because in them the events of that history became permanently effective.

Schlatter, thus, affirmed an historical approach to New Testament theology, but he rejected what he considered the tendency of the major and most influential historical investigations of the New Testament in his time, that is, to combine such an historical approach immediately with a polemic against New Testament Christianity. For him historical investigation of the New Testament was not as neutral as it had been assumed. To begin with, the nature of the New Testament did not permit neutrality because by its very nature it demanded a response of its readers and thus also of the scholar. Furthermore, New Testament theology as an independent discipline did not originate as a neutral enterprise but as an attempt to break free from church doctrine. New thrusts in New Testament theology as an independent historical discipline also characteristically did not come from the investigation of the New Testament itself but from outside.

Although Schlatter considered it necessary that the church should possess a historical presentation of the New Testament, free from the personal views of the interpreter, he nevertheless insisted that the interpreter was unavoidably addressed by the subject matter under consideration. This becomes very clear in his statement that he did not think that there was a more lofty activity for human perception than to recognize what Jesus wanted and said. If an interpretation did not recognize that the New Testament had the form of an address which required a response, it was not historically true to its subject matter. In that regard he considered Calvin's *Institutes* as *historically* more true to the New Testament than most historical investigations.

3. New Testament Theology and Dogmatics

Nevertheless, similar to Gabler, Schlatter was concerned that New Testament theology as an historical discipline had to be distinguished, although not separated, from dogmatics. In contrast with Gabler, however, he did not think that the task of a New Testament theology could have been completed first, independent of dogmatics, and that dogmatics would then begin its task on the firm basis provided by New Testament theology. Because the interpreter was constantly confronted by the appeal made by the New Testament, he or she was continually involved in dogmatic questions. It was, of course, necessary to keep distinguishing dogmatic and historical questions and so avoiding the intertwining of personal views and reactions with the historical investigation. The relationship between historical investigation of the New Testament and dogmatics, thus, according to Schlatter, was not one of dependence but of dialectical interaction.

The task of historical inquiry was to ask what had once been true, without concern for what it might mean in the present. The task of dogmatics was to ask how that which had meaning in the past still determined our thoughts and our will today. But without a sensitivity for the questions of dogmatics, historical inquiry would be lifeless; it would not be able to understand the New Testament because the New Testament was characterized by similar dogmatic questions—even though, of course, of the past. On the other hand, without the relationship to the past provided by the historical inquiry of New Testament theology, dogmatics became exceedingly individualized and arbitrary. Schlatter referred to Friedrich Schleiermacher as an example of such a dogmatics.

According to Schlatter, it was not the task of dogmatics to describe a personal self-consciousness. It had to ask how the past life as presented in the New Testament could become relevant for the present. Dogmatics did not concern the personal convictions of the individual but the knowledge, shared by many, which positively established their faith and by means of which they became bound together. It was by definition a *church* dogmatics, as Karl Barth subsequently formulated. In that regard, Schlatter maintained, dogmatics and New Testament theology were not different formally because from the beginning the New Testament proclamation also functioned to establish the same kind of community, not only by common activity in cult and ethics but also by a common understanding, a common theology. Dogmatics and New Testament theology, thus, did not differ in the sense of only the former having been concerned with dogmatic questions, since both of them were. They also did not differ in the sense that only the former was systematic, since also the latter was a systematic historical presentation. The only really fundamental difference between the two was that New Testament theology as an historical discipline was concerned with the past, which was unrepeatable, whereas dogmatics was concerned with how that past related to the present.

Schlatter also reaffirmed the intention of Gabler's program by rejecting the tendency to take New Testament theology as the only and final function of theology, as if there was no need for a second theological discipline to complete the task. This tendency manifested itself in two ways: either New Testament Christianity sank into the past as something in which we could no longer be involved

—an obvious reference to the *Religionsgeschichtliche* school— or New Testament theology alone was sufficient to itself, the rest being merely a question of Christian living. In neither case, but for different reasons, was there need for dogmatics as a separate task. Like Gabler, Schlatter took the task of a theology of the New Testament to be incomplete without a continuation in dogmatics as a distinguishable discipline.

For Schlatter, however, unlike Gabler, the task of dogmatics was not philosophical, clearly distinguishable from the simplicity of the religious thought of the New Testament. In the sense of his own definition of the term, New Testament thought was already theological, and dogmatics was theological in the same sense. Related to this, Schlatter's program differed in another very important respect from Gabler's. The task of New Testament theology was to establish what the piety of the first period had been. It was not its task to indicate what elements from that piety were relevant for all times, as Gabler had intended with his pure biblical theology. His concern thus was limited to what Gabler had called true biblical theology. He was not concerned with the eternal truths of a pure biblical theology. For Schlatter all theology remained fundamentally historical. New Testament theology and dogmatics in that sense were both historical, involved as they were with the history of Jesus as the revelation of God. It was the task of New Testament theology to present that history, and dogmatics was a result of the response to that history.

4. Schlatter's Method of Interpretation: Statistics and Etiology

Schlatter's actual method of interpretation was characterized by what he called statistics and etiology. Statistics was similar to the two stages of Gabler's true biblical theology, the gathering of all the conceptions present in the New Testament and their systematic ordering according to their internal relationships or differences. But, whereas for Gabler the second step in a biblical theology was the elimination of all contingent aspects of the biblical material, Schlatter's program affirmed precisely certain historically contingent aspects, although not specifically those which Gabler wanted to eliminate. The task of etiology, Schlatter's second step, was to determine how the New Testament concepts and their internal relationships developed. Decisively important was that the sources of the development had to be sought within the framework of the New Testament history itself, not outside of it.

The most important causal factor was the history of Jesus. The question thus was merely whether the church was a further development on the basis of that history, or whether other external features also entered into the picture. Furthermore, it must be asked whether the continued development was to be understood in the sense of a common dependence on a single tradition, that is, of Jesus, or whether the New Testament writers were dependent on each other. In the latter case chronology would have been an important factor as a means of determining who had been dependent on whom, although, Schlatter noted, a view that came to expression in a specific New Testament writing may have been older than the author in whose writing it was encountered. In that regard he was well aware that the New Testament writings were the literary manifestations of an underlying history. Nevertheless, he considered the New Testament history as a development that had been closed off in itself. Understandably, thus, he reaffirmed the solidarity of the canon, and although he did consider it useful to pay attention to the contemporary religions as a means to a better understanding of the New Testament, he did not consider it correct to interpret the New Testament within the context of these religions as the *Religionsgeschichtliche* school had done. The New Testament had to be interpreted from the center of its own development. Schlatter's understanding of New Testament theology, notwithstanding its great complexity as presented in the two volumes of his *Theology of the New Testament*, was of an internally coherent development with the history of Jesus at its center.

5. *Schlatter and the Reformation*

With Schlatter New Testament theology returned full swing to a reaffirmation of those Reformation principles which gave rise to biblical theology and ultimately to New Testament theology as an individual discipline. He did this, however, at a much deeper level of awareness of what had been involved than had been the case in the Reformation—even though his appreciative reference to the historical value of Calvin's *Institutes* suggests that he did not claim to have achieved greater clarity than had been attained by the Reformers.

The Reformers asserted the historical separation of the Bible from the contemporary life of the church as the norm by means of which it could be judged and renewed. At the same time they asserted that all Christian thought had to be biblical. As the implications of this were worked out by historical criticism, culminating in the work of the *Religionsgeschichtliche* school, it became increasingly clear that the thinking of the biblical writers was alien to contemporary thought, which made it difficult to see how the Bible could continue to function as the norm of contemporary life and thought.

In full awareness of this, Schlatter reasserted the Reformation views and at the same time affirmed the necessity of historical inquiry. Indeed it was historical inquiry that had to make clear the historical separation of New Testament thought from present self-consciousness but then also help bridge the historical gap which separated the New Testament from present Christianity. Historical inquiry functioned not only to reveal the historical distance but also to disclose the line of continuity which established the connection between the present and the past. The New Testament was historically not an integral part of twentieth century Christian life and thought, but it was an integral part of the life and thought of New Testament Christianity. New Testament theology as a historical discipline had to investigate that life and thought, and to present it as it had been lived and experienced, for the benefit of present Christianity. Then it was the unique task of dogmatics to find the ways in which that life and thought still had relevance for the present. That the thinking of the New Testament writers was not the same as modern thought prevented dogmatics from becoming individual and arbitrary, which was essentially what the Reformers had in mind. The task of dogmatics was not to present an individual contemporary self-consciousness. It had to represent biblical thought.

6. The Significance of Schlatter

With Schlatter historical investigation of the New Testament became at the same time theological interpretation. He did not negate historical inquiry but tried to incorporate it into an interpretation which was responsive to the appeal of the New Testament proclamation. However, he did object to the view that historical inquiry concerning the New Testament could be neutral. Hence, he rejected the validity of those interpretations which were insensitive to the appeal of the New Testament.

All the same, he did consider it necessary to distinguish between New Testament theology, concerned as it was with the past history of New Testament Christianity, and dogmatics, which tried to ascertain how that past became relevant in the present. In that regard he reaffirmed Gabler's distinction between the two and that they were related. However, he considered their relationship as dialectical, not one-directional as Gabler had taken it. While dogmatic questions gave life to historical inquiry, historical inquiry prevented dogmatics from becoming individualistic and arbitrary.

Schlatter's program, thus, was historical by attempting to present the history of New Testament Christianity from within as a past history, the way someone who had been actually involved in it would have presented it. It was a history very much closed off in itself with its own center, inaccessible from the outside, but in a way which was normal to any participant in a religion. It was not the history of New Testament Christianity taken in a larger historical context which would provide a framework within which it could be interpreted. Rather, historical probability with regard to the New Testament could not be tested by extraneous considerations; only internal coherence and persuasiveness provided evidence. Thus it is not surprising that Schlatter held Calvin's *Institutes* to be *historically* more true to the New Testament than the historical investigations of his time. The New Testament had to be seen not as a religious-cultural phenomenon of Hellenistic antiquity but as the history of a past religious movement which was still vitally relevant for a contemporary religious community.

In the work of Schlatter, thus, an important issue came into focus: what was a theology of the New Testament? Was it a theology *of the New Testament* in the sense of being understandable only by its own intention within its own framework, that is, by means of a positive response to its appeal as a religion? Or was it a *theology* in the sense of the teachings of a religion, similar to many others in Hellenistic antiquity, which was only partially reflected in the New Testament and thus understandable only by making use of all available sources and by interpreting it as part of the general religious movements of the period? There should be no question that both approaches could be considered valid. It was possible to view New Testament Christianity from within in a positive response to the appeal of the Christian proclamation. (That approach is considered essential in the case of the study of other world religions.) But it was also possible to view it from the outside as just another religious movement of Hellenistic antiquity. Schlatter reasserted the former approach after the latter had already been practiced so successfully, especially by the *Religionsgeschichtliche* school.

One of the most important features of Schlatter's program is the clarity of its conception. A theology of the New Testament such as he proposed was not a theology in the strict sense of a coherent, logical, necessary system of ideas about God but theology as an integral part of a life of faith in all its aspects. Sharp but correct was his assertion that representing the New Testament writers as if they thought in the abstract way of Greek thinkers leads to a distorted theology of the New Testament. That amounted to claiming that a theology of the

New Testament in the strict sense of the term, "scientific" theology as he proposed to call it, was an impossibility. Of Schlatter one could say what Wrede wrote about Paul: his theology was religion and his religion was theological. In that regard he could legitimately have claimed to have conceived of a theology that was truly *of the New Testament*.

On the other hand, however, by understanding the relationship between historical inquiry and dogmatics as reciprocal, Schlatter once more allowed present-day dogmatic concerns to predetermine the outcome of the historical inquiry. It is correct to say that historical inquiry would not do justice to texts of the kind that we have in the New Testament without some form of engagement with the claims presented in them. But that engagement, if it is to remain true to the standards of historical inquiry, would have to be understood from a perspective that was contemporaneous with the texts themselves and not from the point of view of present-day dogmatics. Schlatter gave up a strictly historical inquiry in his theology of the New Testament. It was not a "pure" biblical theology of the New Testament but a dogmatic theology and should be appreciated as such.

B. THE PROBLEM OF A "PURE" NEW TESTAMENT THEOLOGY: RUDOLF BULTMANN

1. Sachkritik *and Pure Biblical Theology*

Gabler's program for a true biblical theology was in many ways rounded off with regard to the New Testament in different ways by the *Religionsgeschichtliche* school and by Schlatter. What remained unsolved was the question of a pure biblical theology. The *Religionsgeschichtliche* school obviously considered it irrelevant and ruled it out. On at least one point Schlatter and Wrede agreed: there was not a theology in the strict sense of the term in the New Testament. According to Wrede, not even in connection with Paul could one have thought of a theology in the strict, modern sense of the term. Gabler, of course, also did not conceive of such a theology as having been contained in the Bible. It had to be derived from it by eliminating all the contingent conceptions that were gathered and systematically ordered in a true biblical theology.

The intention of a pure biblical theology, however, was carried further by Bultmann's *sach*-critical interpretation of the New Testament writings, that is, an interpretation that was oriented not toward their contingent form but toward their subject matter, not toward their *means* of expression but toward *what* they expressed. As with Gabler, it was, of course, necessary first to achieve clarity about the means of expression before it was possible to move to the deeper level of what it was that was brought to expression.

An important feature in this *sach*-critical interpretation of Bultmann was that it provided the basis for a critique also of the results of that method of interpretation itself without the necessity of stepping outside the framework of the method. So, for example, when he insisted, in agreement with Karl Barth, that the *Sache*, the real subject matter, of 1 Corinthians 15 was not the *last* events that took place at the end of history but the *end* of history itself which occurred at every moment of the individual's encounter with God, he also insisted, in criticism of Barth, that one should note that in speaking of the end of history Paul nevertheless made use of language concerning the last events of history.[17] Bultmann insisted that attention be given not only to *what* was said, the subject matter, but also to the *means* of saying it. This meant, in effect, to emphasize, respectively, the concerns of Gabler's pure biblical theology, as well as true biblical theology. In this way Bultmann's (and Barth's) understanding of the meaning of the passage remained subject to critical scrutiny on the basis of the text itself in accordance with Bultmann's own methodology.

In Bultmann's method of interpretation as expressed in his concern for *Sachkritik*, thus, a tension between subject matter and means of expression was maintained, making it necessary for the interpreter to keep asking on the basis of the means of expression whether the subject matter was accurately discerned. In this way the interpreter could never have the last word but continued to find her- or himself involved in the tension between the subject matter and the means of expression; the interpreter continued to find her- or himself confronted by the text.

2. *Bultmann's Theology of Paul a System of Ideas?*

Like Schlatter, Bultmann understood theology in the sense of the New Testament to have been an integral part of the complete activity of living. In the epilogue of his *Theology of the New Testament* he argued that theological thinking in the New Testament was the exposition of faith; it grew out of the new understanding of God, the world, and humanity which had been given in faith.[18] He rejected

---

17. Cf. Rudolf Bultmann, "Karl Barth, 'Die Auferstehung der Toten,'" *Theologische Blätter* 5 (1926):7–8; now in *Glauben und Verstehen*, 4th ed. (Tübingen: J. C. B. Mohr [Paul Siebeck], 1961), 1:51–52; English translation, "Karl Barth, The Resurrection of the Dead," in *Faith and Understanding*, trans. L. P. Smith (New York: Harper & Row, 1969), pp. 80–81. Note, however, also Barth's fundamental objection against Bultmann's insistence on *Sachkritik* in the preface to the 3d edition of his commentary on Paul's Letter to the Romans.
18. Bultmann, *Theologie des Neuen Testaments*, p. 586; English translation, *Theology of the New Testament*, 2:237.

the Enlightenment understanding which eliminated from consideration everything local, temporal, individual, or particular in order to be left with what was timeless and generally true.[19] Gabler, of course, did have in mind with his pure biblical theology just such an elimination of particular and temporal elements. In that sense, then, Bultmann implicitly denied agreement with Gabler's program.

However, Bultmann's theology of Paul, which, along with that of John, forms the heart of his *Theology of the New Testament,* is not exactly the mere exposition of faith. True, he did consider Paul's thought to have been formulated from the standpoint of faith, including his thoughts about human existence before faith.[20] Nevertheless, Paul's theology was presented by Bultmann in a way that could very appropriately be called a coherent, logical, necessary system of ideas in terms of which every element of our experience concerning God could be interpreted. His presentation of Paul's theology contradicted what he said about Paul as a theologian.

According to Bultmann, Paul did not develop his thoughts on God and Christ, on the world and humanity, theoretically and coherently in a scholarly treatise like a Greek philosopher or a modern theologian. However, that did not mean that he had not been a real theologian. The way in which Paul reduced acute questions that arose in the congregations with whom he corresponded to a single, fundamentally theological one, the way in which he made concrete decisions on the basis of fundamental theological considerations, revealed that his thoughts grew out of a basic theological position. According to Bultmann, however, that position was not developed as the product of theoretical thought in which all encountered phenomena were objectivized into a world system that was perceived from a distance as it had been in Greek thought. The theological thinking of Paul merely raised what had been experienced in faith to the level of clear, conscious knowing.[21]

3. *The Problem of a Systematic Theory*

There is ambivalence in Bultmann's exposition: Paul had a basic theological position out of which he was able to think through acute questions and on the basis of which he could make his decisions. However, that position was not a product of theoretical thought. In the one case, there was obviously a basic theoretical position on the basis of which all experience was interpreted; in the other, experi-

19. Ibid., p. 591; English translation, 2:243.
20. Cf. the two main subdivisions of his discussion of Paul: "Man prior to the revelation of faith" and "under faith."
21. Bultmann, *Theologie,* p. 191; English translation, 1:190.

ence was merely raised to a conscious level of knowing, *Wissen*. The obvious interrelationship between these two modes of knowing makes it difficult to understand why Bultmann denied that the latter was a product of theoretical thought. Presumably one could not speak of raising experience to the level of understanding, *Verstehen*, in the latter case because that would of necessity have had to mean the level of a theory. The reason for Bultmann's ambivalence was his fighting the specter of an objectivized world system which was perceived at a distance, not by the Greeks, as he says, but presumably in the Enlightenment. He did not really react against a system produced by theoretical thought but against the objectification of it in a separate world.

A system of theoretical thought, however, does not have to be in terms of an objectivized world. Such an objectivized world is a fallacy which occurs very commonly in theoretical thinking. Whitehead identified it as the fallacy of misplaced concreteness, that is, the fallacy precisely of mistaking a system of theoretical thought for the concrete world of experience which such a system was supposed to have interpreted. His definition of speculative philosophy reveals very clearly his avoidance of that fallacy. It was "a coherent, logical, necessary system of general ideas in terms of which *every element of our experience* can be *interpreted.*" Thus it may not be altogether surprising that Bultmann's own definition of Paul's theology fits so well the definition of theology we proposed in chapter 1 based on Whitehead's definition of speculative philosophy. The reduction of acute questions to a fundamentally theological one and the making of decisions on the basis of fundamental theological considerations amount to having a coherent, logical, necessary system of general ideas in terms of which every element of our experience concerning matters relating to God can be interpreted. Bultmann did not, of course, understand his interpretation of Paul has having been in terms of timeless concepts in the sense of an objectivized world of ideas but in terms of categories of thought that concerned human existence directly, the so-called existentials. These categories of thought in terms of which Bultmann interpreted Paul, however, were themselves generally valid, and as such they too were timeless concepts or ideas. It is necessary to distinguish between the subject matter of interpretation, which can include features that are contingent, and the means of interpretation, the categories, which have to be universal, timeless if they are to be understandable at all times as Bultmann assumed. As will be seen below, however, there were features also of the subject matter of the

New Testament which, even though not timeless, were nevertheless, according to Bultmann, not contingent in every respect, in the sense that they were valid for human beings at all times.

4. A Theology Based on Paul

And yet Paul was not quite such a theoretical thinker. As Wrede put it, Paul took the first, fundamentally very important step from religion to theology. Paul had not been a theologian in the stricter sense of the term. It was Bultmann who produced a system of thought on the basis of the hints provided by Paul. As is well known, according to Bultmann it was a system that was characterized by the conception that every statement about God was at the same time a statement about humanity. Paul's theology, according to him, was at the same time anthropology, and his presentation of the theology of Paul bears this out. One may argue about the nature of the actual presentation provided by Bultmann, but in principle he has shown that it could be done.

To a certain degree every interpreter of Paul—or any other New Testament writer—does something similar to what Bultmann has done but not nearly with the same consistency. It becomes a problem only when it is then tacitly assumed that Paul, or some other author, actually thought in terms of such a system. It is akin to the fallacy of misplaced concreteness in the sense that the system of thought that had been produced as a means of interpreting Paul's thinking becomes confused with that thinking itself. This fallacy occurs when the two senses of theology are confused, something which happens very easily in the case of Paul for whom both senses apply. For Paul himself, theological thought was an integral part of his total life as a Christian, but he himself never developed his ideas into a coherent, logical system. Nevertheless, he did provide the material on the basis of which such a system could be developed. He probably could have developed it himself if he had been more theoretically inclined. The fallacy occurs when the system of theological ideas based on his thought is projected back onto him as part of his own thinking—when one forgets in which way he was a theologian and in which way he was not.

The occurrence of this fallacy is evident when an interpreter asserts what Paul must have meant in a certain passage because it has to be in agreement with what the interpreter knows (!) as Paul's thinking. A typical passage is Rom. 7:14ff. So, for example, Bultmann knows that the meaning of the passage could not be the "cheap" insight from Ovidius' Metamorphoses 8. 20, "I see and strive for what is better, but reach for what is worst," because the anthropology presupposed by that saying is not the anthropology of Paul.[22] Such reasoning assumes that Paul had a systematic anthropology and that every statement he made was coherent with that anthropology because it was supposed to have been drawn from it. The most Bultmann might have claimed is that if Ovidius' saying was what Paul meant, it would have been inconsistent with what he (Paul) said in other places on the subject of anthropology. But then, it is well known that Paul's writings are full of logical contradictions and inconsistencies which would be a weakness only from the point of view of a coherent, logical system of thought.

5. A Theology behind John

Bultmann's theology of John is not presented in the same way as a theological system of thought, which is probably appropriate since John's writings do not lend themselves to such a systematization. This is particularly interesting since John, of all New Testament writers, may have been the beneficiary of an existing theological system, that is, of the Gnostics.

In the case of John, thus, it would probably be more appropriate to speak of a theology behind John than to attempt to outline a theology based on his writings. It does not appear possible, however, to reconstruct that theology as it might have existed because the material provided by the Gospel and the Letters does not lend itself to such a reconstruction.

6. A "Pure" Theology of the New Testament: Herbert Braun

A step in the direction of a theological system of the New Testament as a whole was taken by Braun, especially in an article on "The Problem of a Theology of the New Testament." Here he expanded the more detailed investigation he had made earlier concerning only Christology in "The Meaning of New Testament Christology" to include also soteriology, attitude toward the Law, eschatology, and the sacraments, drawing also from many of his earlier studies. Braun's method was a consistent implementation of the principles of Bultmann's subject matter oriented, *sachkritische,* method of demythologizing. Characteristic of Braun's method was the compari-

---

22. Rudolf Bultmann, "Römer 7 und die Anthropologie des Paulus," in *Imago Dei: Beiträge zur theologischen Anthropologie. Gustav Krüger zum siebzigsten Geburtstage am 29 Juni 1932 dargebracht,* ed. Heinrich Bornkamm (Giessen: Alfred Töpelmann, 1932), pp. 145–65, esp. p.155; reprinted in Rudolf Bultmann, *Der alte und der neue Mensch in der Theologie des Paulus, Libelli* 98 (Darmstadt: Wissenschaftliche Buchgesellschaft, 1964), pp. 28–40, esp. p. 31; also in *Exegetica: Aufsätze zur Erforschung des Neuen Testaments,* ed. Erich Dinkler (Tübingen: J. C. B. Mohr [Paul Siebeck]), pp. 198–209, esp. p. 201.

son of the understanding of the New Testament writers with the views concerning similar topics expressed in the contemporary religions and in the popular philosophy of the time. In these comparisons he attempted to distinguish between the common thought-forms of the religious and popular philosophical thinking of the time and the distinctive thoughts that were brought to expression in them. Such comparisons required, of course, sensitivity not only to the distinctiveness of Christianity but also to that of the other religions and popular philosophy. That, according to Braun, was what de-mythologizing was all about: the distinction between the religious and popular philosophical thought-forms of the time and the *actual* thoughts expressed by means of them.

In the case of "The Problem of a Theology of the New Testament," this method of comparison and discrimination of differences was supplemented by an attempt to determine the trends of the development within Christianity in connection with the abovementioned five topics. According to Braun's analysis, there was a tendency in each case to become less dependent on the thought-forms of the time and to address the subject matter increasingly directly. Consequently, he concluded that the characteristic feature of New Testament Christianity was the conception of a god who found the human being acceptable as she or he was, whereas it had been characteristic of all the other religions, Jewish as well as pagan, and of popular philosophy to attempt to guide humanity to a higher level of acceptability before the deity. In an age in which the common desire was to escape from the desperate situation in the world by some kind of participation in a divine existence, Christianity proclaimed the acceptability of a person in her or his existence as a human being. By implication that also meant an affirmation of the world.

What Braun produced was, of course, not yet a comprehensive theological system based on the New Testament, but the basic principles which he identified could serve to interpret every element of our experience concerning God. And even though these principles were not yet coherently articulated in New Testament Christianity, Braun's interpretation suggests that they had actually functioned as a system of ideas in terms of which New Testament Christianity interpreted its experience of matters relating to God. What Braun identified as the basic characteristic of New Testament Christianity was also not representative of all of the New Testament. It was the underlying, developing system of fundamental ideas which characterized New Testament Christianity that interested him. Similarly, when he asked for the meaning, *der Sinn*, of New Testament Christology, he did not ask for a meaning which encompassed all of

New Testament Christology but only what it was that was meaningful, that made sense, in it. What Braun pointed to was not a *true* but a *pure* theology of the New Testament, in the sense of Gabler's distinction.

CONCLUSION

As Schlatter produced what was akin to a true theology of the New Testament, Bultmann produced something akin to a pure theology, not of the New Testament but of Paul. Neither of these theologies can be accepted as *contained in* the New Testament. They were derived from it. In the case of Braun's theology of the New Testament, which was not presented as a comprehensive system but only as the basic principles of such a system, one might be able to claim that it actually functioned in a tacit way in New Testament Christianity; these principles were the means by which New Testament Christianity interpreted every element of its experience concerning God.

Something similar would have been true for Paul, and in his case at a more conscious and intentional level, however, not the level of theoretical development as presented by Bultmann. Bultmann, in denying that Paul's theology was a system of theoretical thought, probably also did not consider his own theology of Paul as such a theoretical system, and it was indeed not theoretical in the sense of an objectivized world system that was perceived from a distance. It was, however, theoretical in Whitehead's sense of a coherent, logical, necessary system in terms of which our experience of matters relating to God could be interpreted. But Paul himself had not developed his theology theoretically to the level presented by Bultmann. Bultmann's theology of Paul may more appropriately be called a theology not of Paul, but based on Paul, that is, a theology developed theoretically by Bultmann on the basis of hints provided by Paul.

In the case of John, Bultmann did not provide such a theological system. John also does not appear to provide the basis on which such a system could be developed. On the other hand, there may have been a well-developed (Gnostic) system of theology behind John out of which his thoughts were drawn. The Gospel and Letters of John, however, also do not appear to provide the material out of which that system could be reconstructed.

The one question which remains unresolved is whether a pure theology of the New Testament, in the sense of a comprehensive system based on the New Testament as a whole, can be developed. The answer to that question will be found only when such a system has been attempted. Braun has at least indicated one possible way in which one might proceed with such an enterprise.

The "pure" New Testament theology of Bultmann and of Braun was unlike that conceived by Gabler in that they did not attempt to identify those elements in the New Testament which were noncontingent and universally valid. But Bultmann and Braun did act in the spirit of Gabler in their efforts to identify a dimension in the New Testament which was not merely historically conditioned, that is, limited to the ancient world. That dimension constituted what could be called their "pure" New Testament theology. It was defined by two characteristics, both of which were necessary: (1) It had to be congruent with what the New Testament writers meant and not merely with what they said, a distinction that was made possible by *Sachkritik*, an interpretation that was oriented distinctively toward the subject matter of the text. (2) It had to be relevant for the contemporary interpreter in such a way that she or he could find herself or himself addressed by it.

The subject matter of the New Testament as interpreted by Bultmann and Braun, thus, was not a body of timeless truths. However, they did assume that it was relevant for all human beings at all times, that is, they assumed that human beings remained, as human beings, *fundamentally* the same and that insofar as the subject matter of the New Testament addressed the human being at this fundamental level, it remained valid for all times.

Bultmann showed a way in which it was possible to interpret the engagement with New Testament texts from a perspective that was contemporaneous with the New Testament itself, by means of *Sachkritik*, the distinction between the subject matter and its means of expression in a text. However, the questions with which the interpreter approached the text to begin the process of interpretation once more provided a way in which dogmatics could predetermine the meaning of the text. Bultmann tried to prevent this by distinguishing between prejudice and preunderstanding, that is, between a (dogmatic) bias which was maintained throughout the process of interpretation and the (informed) expectation with which the text was approached in a process of interpretation that remained open-minded.[23] Nevertheless, that did not prevent these initial questions from setting certain limits within which the process of interpretation had to take place. In some way the hold which these initial questions had on the interpretation had to be broken.

23. Cf., e.g., Rudolf Bultmann, "Ist voraussetzungslose Exegese möglich?" *Theologische Zeitschrift* 13(1957): 409–17; now in *Glauben und Vestehen*, 2d ed. (Tübingen: J. C. B. Mohr [Paul Siebeck], 1962), 3: 142–50; English translation, "Is Exegesis without Presuppositions Possible?" *Existence and Faith: Shorter Writings of Rudolf Bultmann*, selected, translated, and introduced by Schubert Ogden (New York: Meridian Books [Living Age Books LA 29], 1960), pp. 289–96.

This is what was accomplished by Braun when he placed the emphasis back on what had been the issue in the situation of the texts themselves, that is, by comparing the New Testament expressions with those of other texts of the same period. In the attempt to discern the distinctive characteristics of the various texts by such comparison, the interpreter was forced to recognize the original questions to which the texts were attempted responses, and so she or he could become challenged once more by the original claims that were presented in the texts. The interchange between the ancient texts themselves, Christian as well as non-Christian, uncovered the original questions to which the texts were attempted answers as well as the distinctive claims presented by the texts. The preunderstanding, represented by the set of questions with which the text was approached, was not completely eliminated in this way, but by viewing the text within the framework of other related texts, additional leverage was provided, that is, in addition to that provided by the text itself, by means of which the hold of the preunderstanding, which could easily become entrenched as a dogmatic bias, could be broken—which was fundamentally what Gabler had intended. Thus the task of a pure biblical theology as envisaged by Gabler was carried out, but in a way which he himself had not been able to envisage.

In a general way Bultmann had given an indication of this kind of method in *Primitive Christianity in its Contemporary Setting*,[24] as the title indicates. In a sense the method was merely a radicalization of the *Religionsgeschichtliche* school's program of interpreting the New Testament within the framework of the religions of the time. What Bultmann, and, methodologically more consistently, Braun, wanted was that the interpreter should recognize that the intention in these texts was to engage the readers, as Schlatter had insisted. At the same time, in contrast with Schlatter and in agreement with the intentions of the *Religionsgeschichtliche* school, they maintained that the nature of the engagement could have been discerned properly only if it took into account the perspectives on those texts that were contemporaneous with the texts themselves. In agreement with the *Religionsgeschichtliche* school, Braun went even further by suggesting that that was the only perspective from out of which the texts became understandable.[25]

24. Rudolf Bultmann, *Das Urchristentum im Rahmen der antiken Religion* (Zürich: Artemis-Verlag, 1949); English translation, *Primitive Christianity in its Contemporary Setting*, trans. Reginald H. Fuller (Cleveland: World Publishing Co., 1956).
25. For a limited attempt at this kind of an interpretation, cf. my "Contemporary Significance of the New Testament," *Journal of the American Academy of Religion* 45(1977): 1–33.

Epilogue:
The Significance of
New Testament
Theology

New Testament theology has its roots in the Reformation understanding that the Bible was not an integral part of the contemporary life and thought of the church but belonged to the historical past. The Reformers intended to establish the Bible as the sole base and norm over against the contemporary church by means of which to judge and renew it, but by setting it apart from the contemporary life and thought of the church, the Reformers set a process in motion which made it increasingly questionable how a collection of documents from the past could be normative for the present. The history of New Testament theology is a history of trying to answer that question, in principle as well as in practice.

The outlines for the range of possible ways of answering the question were already given programmatically by Gabler with his distinction between biblical theology in a broader and in a narrower sense, or, especially, true and pure biblical theology, as the means of making the religious thinking of the Bible available to contemporary dogmatics in the form of a theology. It was the former, more historically oriented task which received most attention in the period that followed, culminating in the contrasting conceptions of it in the *Religionsgeschichtliche* school, represented in that regard particularly by Wrede and Bousset, on the one hand, and almost individually by Schlatter, on the other. Wrede and Bousset showed that the New Testament writings could be understood as products of the developing primitive Christian religion and that that religion could be investigated like any other religion of Hellenistic antiquity. Schlatter, on the other hand, proved that it was also possible to approach the New Testament historically from the inside by responding to its appeal, as a New Testament Christian might have done.

Both approaches have validity, each laying bare different aspects of the New Testament. The fact that the *Religionsgeschichtliche* school identified the New Testament writings as religious documents, whereas Schlatter understood the New Testament as a theological collection, is of little consequence since Schlatter's understanding of theology in the New Testament sense was really not very different from what Wrede and others meant by a religion. The real difference is that the *Religionsgeschichtliche* school approached the New Testament from the outside as the object of critical historical scrutiny, whereas Schlatter approached it from the inside as one who participated in the primitive Christian religion would have done. The result was that Schlatter did not need a second discipline, such as Gabler's pure biblical theology, to mediate between his (true) New Testament theology and the contemporary task of dogmatics because the two were dialectically related all along. For Schlatter the historical separation of the New Testament from the present was overcome by recognition of the appeal made by it and to which the contemporary Christian had to respond.

As the object of historical-critical scrutiny in the *Religionsgeschichtliche* school, however, the New Testament was surrendered to the past. The New Testament writings were understood to have spoken to their own time and not to have been intended for the present. A historical interpretation could only clarify the significance of the New Testament writings for their own time, which was so different from our own that it could merely serve to bring out all the more the historical distance which separated it from us. If the New Testament were to have relevance also for the present, the question of what the New Testament writings meant in their own time would have had to be followed by another, namely, what was meaningful in them for more than just their own time. That was the task which Gabler had set for a pure biblical theology.

An attempt to carry out that task was made by Bultmann with his program of subject-oriented interpretation, in which he tried to distinguish between what was said and what was meant, between the contemporary thought-forms of the New Testament writings and the subject matter expressed by means of those thought-forms. His *Theology of the New Testament,* especially the part(s) on the theology of Paul and of John, is an important product of that attempt at interpretation. In the theology of Paul, Bultmann presented the thoughts of Paul in the form of a theology in the strict sense of a coherent, logical, necessary system of ideas in terms of which a contemporary Christian could interpret every element of his or her experience concerning matters relating to God, even though he may not have wanted to call it a theology in that sense. Bultmann did not present a theology of the New Testament as a whole. His *Theology of the New Testament* is a combination of a history of the development of the primitive Christian religion and a theology of Paul and of John.

Braun attempted to identify at least some principles that might be involved in such a theology of the New Testament as a whole. Whether such a theology of the New Testament can actually be produced remains to be seen. The most basic methodological principle suggested by Braun was that the engagement with the New Testament texts should take place not within the framework of present-day meanings but within the framework provided especially by other texts from Hellenistic antiquity. It was the framework provided by such contemporary texts which made it possible to distinguish the subject matter and the means of expression in the New Testament texts, which is the task of a pure biblical theology of the New Testament. After that, one could perform the dogmatic task of interpreting the subject matter of the New Testament discerned in this way in doctrines that are relevant for the present.

The question how the collection of documents from Hellenistic antiquity which we call the New Testament could be normative for the present continues to motivate most, if not all, New Testament scholarship even though it has become fashionable to deny that it is so. If it were not the case, the great effort that goes into that kind of scholarship would be incomprehensible. A theology is the culmination of the attempt to answer that question. All of this being the case, Gabler's program for the comprehensive theological task, and the way it was worked out in further detail and depth by Wrede, Bousset, Schlatter, Bultmann, and Braun, may serve as a guide for locating within that comprehensive task the work done by others concerning the New Testament and giving meaning to it. This applies not only to other theologies of the New Testament but to all other work done in the area of New Testament studies, including the detailed investigations of the most isolated subjects. The annotations in the bibliography which follows spell that out in the case of some of the most directly relevant investigations.

Annotated Bibliography

A. THEORETICAL WORKS ON THE PROBLEM OF A THEOLOGY
OF THE NEW TESTAMENT

BAUR, FERDINAND CHRISTIAN. *Vorlesungen über neutestamentliche Theologie*. Edited by Ferdinand Friedrich Baur. Leipzig: Fues's Verlag (L. W. Reisland), 1864. Reprinted with an introduction by Werner Georg Kümmel. Darmstadt: Wissenschaftliche Buchgesellschaft, 1973. Baur's lectures on New Testament theology, posthumously published by his son. It is presented as the beginning of the history of doctrine and represents Baur's thoroughly historical interpretation of the New Testament. Cf. the discussion above in chap. 3, A, 1–2.

BOUSSET, WILHELM. *Kyrios Christos: Geschichte des Christusglaubens von den Anfängen des Christentums bis Irenaeus*. Göttingen: Vandenhoeck & Ruprecht, 1913. 5th edition, with an introductory word by Rudolf Bultmann, 1965. English translation, *Kyrios Christos: A History of the Belief in Christ from the Beginnings of Christianity to Irenaeus*. Translated by John E. Steely. Nashville: Abingdon Press, 1970. The most thorough presentation to date of the history of the developing primitive Christian religion within the framework of its environment. The central focus is on the cult of Christ the Lord. Cf. the discussion above in chap. 3, C.

BRAUN, HERBERT. "Die Problematik einer Theologie des Neuen Testaments." *Zeitschrift für Theologie und Kirche* 58(1961): 3–18. Reprinted in *Gesammelte Studien zum Neuen Testament*. Tübingen: J. C. B. Mohr (Paul Siebeck), 1962, pp. 325–41. English translation, "The Problem of a Theology of the New Testament." Translated by Jack T. Sanders. *Journal for Theology and the Church* 1(1965): 169–83. Reprinted in Altizer, Thomas J. J., ed. *Toward a New Christianity*. New York: Harcourt, Brace and World, 1967, pp. 201–15.

———. "Der Sinn der neutestamentlichen Christologie." *Zeitschrift für Theologie und Kirche* 54(1957): 341–77. Reprinted in *Gesammelte Studien zum Neuen Testament*. Tübingen: J. C. B. Mohr (Paul Siebeck), 1962, pp. 86–99. English translation, "The Meaning of the Christology of the

New Testament." Translated by Paul J. Achtemeier. *Journal for Theology and the Church* 5(1968): 89–127. Two of the most significant contributions of Braun on the subject of New Testament theology, representing his method of deriving the distinctive meanings of writings by comparing them with others, Christian as well as non-Christian, that share similar concerns. Cf. the discussion above in chap. 4, B, 6.

BULTMANN, RUDOLF. "Das Problem einer theologischen Exegese des Neuen Testaments." *Zwischen den Zeiten* 3(1925): 334–57. Reprinted in Strecker, Georg, ed. *Das Problem der Theologie des Neuen Testaments*, pp. 249–77.

————. "Neues Testament und Mythologie." In *Kerygma und Mythos*, edited by H. -W. Bartsch, pp. 15–48. Hamburg: Herbert Reich, 1948. 2d edition 1951. English translation, "The New Testament and Mythology." In *Kerygma and Myth*, vol. 1. Translated by R. H. Fuller, pp. 1–44. London: SPCK, 1953. Two essays in which Bultmann discusses a subject matter oriented interpretation of the New Testament in which a distinction is made between what was said and what was meant. It is of particular significance that the 1925 essay already expresses the essential ideas of the famous programmatic essay on demythologizing, without yet making use of this latter conception. Cf. the discussion above in chap. 4, B, 1.

CHILDS, BREVARD S. *Biblical Theology in Crisis*. Philadelphia: Westminster Press, 1970.

————. *The Book of Exodus: A Critical, Theological Commentary*. Philadelphia: Westminster Press, 1974. Childs proposes that for an understanding of the biblical text, the canon itself should be taken as the context within which the interpretation takes place. It should be noted that such a method of interpretation makes sense only when the canon is taken as the framework within which faith is capable of moving and developing itself. It would make no sense if the canon is taken as an external rule of faith by means of which true and false faith can be distinguished. Relevant is the discussion above in chap. 1, B, 2–4.

DEISSMANN, ADOLF. "Zur Methode der biblischen Theologie des Neuen Testaments." *Zeitschrift für Theologie und Kirche* 3(1893): 126–39. Reprinted in Strecker, Georg, ed. *Das Problem der Theologie des Neuen Testaments*. pp. 67–80. An early address in which Deissmann already proposes that the New Testament had to be interpreted within the framework of its environment. Cf. the discussion above in chap. 3, A, 3.

EBELING, GERHARD. "Was heisst 'Biblische Theologie'?" In *Wort und Glaube*, vol. 1. Tübingen: J. C. B. Mohr (Paul Siebeck), 1960, pp. 69–89. 2d edition 1962. English translation, "The Meaning of 'Biblical Theology.'" In *Word and Faith*. Translated by J. W. Leitch. Philadelphia: Fortress Press, 1960, pp. 79–97. The original publication of the actual address in the *Journal of Theological Studies* 6(1955): 210–25 is a very unsatisfactory English version. Ebeling discusses a variety of very important issues in connection with biblical theology from the point of view of a systematic theologian. It includes a brief but very perceptive history of the discipline. Cf. the discussion above in chap. 1.

GABLER, JOHANN PHILIPP. "Oratio de iusto discrimine theologiae biblicae et dogmaticae regundisque recte utriusque finibus." Inaugural address in Altdorf, 30 March 1787. Published in *Opuscula academica*, edited by Th. A. Gabler and J. G. Gabler, vol. 1. Ulm: 1831, pp. 179–94. German translation, "Von der richtigen Unterscheidung der biblischen und der dogmatischen Theologie und der rechten Bestimmung ihrer beider Ziele." Translated by Otto Merk. In *Biblische Theologie des Neuen Testaments in ihrer Anfangszeit*, pp. 272–84. Reprinted in Strecker, Georg. *Das Problem der Theologie des Neuen Testaments*, pp. 32–44. The inaugural address which may still be the single most significant discussion of biblical theology. It was intended as a program for the development of a separate discipline of biblical theology as part of the comprehensive theological task which also included dogmatic theology. Particularly useful is the clear perception of the distinctive features of the various aspects of the comprehensive theological task. Cf. the discussion above in chap. 2.

GILKEY, LANGDON. "Cosmology, Ontology, and the Travail of Biblical Language." *Journal of Religion* 41(1961): 194–205. In a penetrating analysis, Gilkey argues that biblical theology no longer considers the Bible as the description of God's acts and words but as a book of Hebrew religion, even in the case of scholars such as G. Ernest Wright and Bernhard Anderson who claim to be writing about the acts of God. According to Gilkey, what is needed is an ontology which would make it once more meaningful to speak of the God who acted. The unquestioned assumption is that somehow God did act. Relevant is the discussion above in chap. 3, A, 3, and B, C.

GÜTTGEMANNS, ERHARDT. "Linguistisch-literaturwissenschaftliche Grundlegung einer neutestamentlichen Theologie." *Linguistica Biblica* 13/14(1972): 2–18. English translation, "Linguistic-Literary Critical Foundation of a New Testament Theology." Translated by William G. Doty. "Erhardt Güttgemanns' 'Generative Poetics.'" *Semeia*, vol. 6. Edited by Norman R. Petersen. Missoula, Mont.: The Society of Biblical Literature, 1976, pp. 181–215. Güttgemanns emphasizes the deeper levels of language in the formulation of New Testament thought. The reasoning is very compact, in the form of forty-seven interrelated theses, but it is nevertheless one of the presentations of Güttgemanns which might be more readily understandable by someone unfamiliar with contemporary linguistics and with the author's frequently highly individual forms of expression. Although Güttgemanns tends to understand all thought as emerging from grammar in what could be called a pan-grammatism, this remains a highly significant contribution.

HASEL, GERHARD F. *Old Testament Theology: Basic Issues in the Current Debate*. Grand Rapids: William B. Eerdmans Publishing Co., 1972. Revised edition, 1975. A well-written discussion of the subject, much of which is also of interest for the New Testament student. It is more a survey than a critical uncovering of the fundamental issues.

KÄHLER, MARTIN. *Der sogenannte historische Jesus und der geschichtliche, biblische Christus.* Leipzig: A. Deichertschen Verlagsbuchhandlung, 1892. Republished and edited by E. Wolff, 2d expanded edition, München: Chr. Kaiser Verlag, 1956. English translation, *The So-called Historical Jesus and the Historic Biblical Christ.* Translated by C. E. Braaten. Philadelphia: Fortress Press, 1964. A work which deservedly became very influential in the recent past. Kähler argues convincingly that historical research is not the most appropriate way of uncovering the meaning of Christ for the believing community. It is important to note that "historical" for Kähler does not refer to the Jesus who actually lived, but to "Jesus" as a construction of historical inquiry. The only access to the real Jesus is through the effect which he had on his followers and as presented in the New Testament writings. Relevant is the discussion above in chap. 2, 6.

KÄSEMANN, ERNST. "The Problem of a New Testament Theology." *New Testament Studies* 19(1973): 235–45. A brief critical discussion of the history of New Testament theology and of some of the current works on the subject. He reaffirms the position of Schlatter which he formulates succinctly: "With Schlatter, I regard the revelation of Christ in its progress and varied interpretation as the real clue to the New Testament." Relevant is the discussion above in chap. 4.

KRAUS, HANS-JOACHIM. *Die Biblische Theologie: Ihre Geschichte und Problematik.* Neukirchen-Vluyn: Neukirchener Verlag, 1970. The most comprehensive discussion of the subject. According to Kraus, the subject matter of a biblical theology is not God and humanity in isolation but the encounter and community between them as initiated by God himself and effected in the act or acts of revelation.

KÜMMEL, WERNER GEORG. *Das Neue Testament: Geschichte der Erforschung seiner Probleme.* Freiburg/München: Verlag Karl Alber, 1958. English translation, *The New Testament: The History of the Investigation of its Problems.* Translated by S. McLean Gilmour and Howard C. Kee. Nashville: Abingdon Press, 1972. This is basically a sourcebook, with interpretive comments by Kümmel to indicate the lines of development. The selection of the material strongly favors a development toward an increasingly thorough historical interpretation. It is misleading in the English version that the source materials are in small print and Kümmel's comments in large print. An indispensable work for New Testament study.

MERK, OTTO. *Biblische Theologie des Neuen Testaments in ihrer Anfangszeit.* Marburg: N. G. Elwert Verlag, 1972. A thorough discussion of the work on biblical theology by Johann Philipp Gabler and Georg Lorenz Bauer. The investigation is strongly biased in favor of a thoroughly historical interpretation, which stands to a certain degree in the way of a true understanding of, especially, Gabler. Cf. above the discussion of Gabler in chap. 2.

REITZENSTEIN, RICHARD. *Die hellenistischen Mysterienreligionen nach ihren Grundgedanken und Wirkungen.* Stuttgart: Verlag B. G. Teubner, 1910. Reprint of the 3d edition of 1927. Darmstadt: Wissenschaftliche

Buchgesellschaft E. V., 1956. English translation, *Hellenistic Mystery-Religions: Their Basic Ideas and Significance.* Translated by John E. Steely. Pittsburgh, Pa.: Pickwick Press, 1978. One of the most revealing presentations of the setting out of which primitive Christianity emerged. It is not a commentary on the New Testament, but one may learn more about the New Testament from this work than from most commentaries and monographs on the New Testament writings themselves. Relevant are the discussions above in chap. 3 and in chap. 4, B, 6.

SCHLATTER, ADOLF. *Die Theologie des Neuen Testaments und die Dogmatik.* Gütersloh: Verlag von C. Bertelsmann, 1909. Reprinted in Schlatter, Adolf. *Zur Theologie des Neuen Testaments und zur Dogmatik: Kleine Schriften.* With an introductory word by Ulrich Luck. München: Chr. Kaiser Verlag, 1969, pp. 203–55. Also in Strecker, Georg, ed. *Das Problem der Theologie des Neuen Testaments,* pp. 155–214. English translation, "The Theology of the New Testament and Dogmatics." Translated by Robert Morgan. *The Nature of New Testament Theology.* London: SCM Press / Naperville, Ill.: Alec R. Allenson, 1973, pp. 117–66. The theoretical discussion of the principles on which his own *Theologie des Neuen Testaments* is based. According to Schlatter, the only appropriate approach to the New Testament is in terms of a dialectic between dogmatic concern and historical distance, the former to ensure an openness to the message of the New Testament, the latter to avoid dogmatic subjectivity. The principles discussed in the essay remain influential in all subsequent attempts at a theological interpretation of the New Testament, even where the influence of Schlatter himself is not recognized. Cf. the discussion above in chap. 4, A.

————. *Die Theologie des Neuen Testaments.* 2 vols. Calw und Stuttgart: Verlag des Vereinsbuchhandlung, 1909–10.

SCHMID, CHRISTIAN FRIEDRICH. *Biblische Theologie des Neuen Testaments.* Edited by C. Weizsäcker. Leipzig: Fr. Richter, 1853. English translation, *Biblical Theology of the New Testament.* Translated by H. G. Venables. Edinburgh: T. & T. Clark, 1877. An early work in which the author attempted to interpret the theology of the New Testament in the total context of the life of primitive Christianity. Cf. the discussion above in chap. 3, A, 2.

STRECKER, GEORG, ed. *Das Problem der Theologie des Neuen Testaments.* Darmstadt: Wissenschaftliche Buchgesellschaft, 1975. A collection of some of the most significant writings on the problem of a theology of the New Testament, with an informative introductory discussion by Strecker.

WEISS, JOHANNES. *Die Predigt Jesu vom Reiche Gottes.* Göttingen: Vandenhoeck & Ruprecht, 1900. 3d edition by Ferdinand Hahn, with an introductory word by Rudolf Bultmann, 1964. English translation, *Jesus' Proclamation of the Kingdom of God.* Translated by Richard Hyde Hiers and David Larrimore Holland. Philadelphia: Fortress Press, 1971. The pioneering work in which Weiss conclusively showed that Jesus' conception of the kingdom of God was understandable only within the framework of Jewish apocalypticism. Cf. the discussion above in chap. 3, C, 3.

WREDE, WILLIAM. *Über Aufgabe und Methode der sogenannten neutestamentlichen Theologie*. Göttingen: Vandenhoeck & Ruprecht, 1897. Reprinted in Strecker, Georg, ed. *Das Problem der Theologie des Neuen Testaments*, pp. 81–154. English translation, "The Task and Methods of 'New Testament Theology.'" Translated by Robert Morgan. In *The Nature of New Testament Theology*. London: SCM Press / Naperville Ill.: Alec R. Allenson, 1973, pp. 68–116. A programmatic essay which clarifies the necessity for an interpretation of the New Testament as part of the history of primitive Christian religion and theology and outlines the way in which such an interpretation might proceed. Cf. the discussion above in chap. 3, B.

————. *Paulus*. Halle: 1904. 2d edition with a preface by Wilhelm Bousset. Tübingen: J. C. B. Mohr (Paul Siebeck), 1907. English translation, *Paul*. Translated by Edward Lummis. Lexington, Ky.: American Theological Library Association Committee on Reprinting, 1962. A monograph on Paul in which Wrede also deals specifically with the problem of Paul as a theologian. Cf. the discussion above in chap. 3, B, 10.

B. SELECTED CURRENT THEOLOGIES OF THE NEW TESTAMENT

BONSIRVEN, JOSEPH, S. J. *Théologie du Nouveau Testament*. Paris: Editions Montaigne, 1951. English translation, *Theology of the New Testament*. Translated by S. F. L. Tye. Westminster: Newman Press / London: Burns and Oates, 1963. A Roman Catholic work with the stated premise that an approach from the point of view of the Christian believer is advantageous.

BULTMANN, RUDOLF. *Theologie des Neuen Testaments*. Tübingen: Verlag J. C. B. Mohr (Paul Siebeck), 1948–53. 3d edition 1958. English translation, *The Theology of the New Testament*. Translated by Kendrick Grobel. 2 vols. New York: Charles Scribner's Sons, 1951–55. This is really a history of primitive Christian religion *and theology* revealing the influence of Bousset's *Kyrios Christos* in form as well as conception. The central part on Paul and John is explicitly theological.

CONZELMANN, HANS. *Grundriss der Theologie des Neuen Testaments*. München: Chr. Kaiser Verlag, 1967. English translation, *An Outline of the Theology of the New Testament*. Translated by John Bowden. New York: Harper & Row, 1967. Conzelmann understands his New Testament theology as "the exposition of the original *texts* of faith, that is, of the oldest formulations of the credo." In that regard it is reminiscent, although not a carrying out, of the attempt by Paul Feine (*Die Gestalt des apostolischen Glaubensbekenntnisses in der Zeit des Neuen Testaments*. Leipzig: Dörfling & Franke, 1925) to uncover an original credo which he believed the resurrected Christ had given to his disciples.

CULLMANN, OSCAR. *Christus und die Zeit: Die Urchristliche Zeit- und Geschichtsauffassung*. Zollikon/Zürich: Evangelischer Verlag, A. G., 1946. English translation, *Christ and Time: The Primitive Christian Conception of Time and History*. Translated by Floyd Filson. Philadelphia: Westminster Press, 1964.

————. *Heil als Geschichte: Heilsgeschichtliche Existenz im Neuen Testa-*

ment. Tübingen: J. C. B. Mohr (Paul Siebeck), 1965. English translation, *Salvation in History.* Translated by Sidney G. Sowers. New York: Harper & Row, 1967. Both of these represent Cullmann's fundamental understanding that the basic theological conception in the New Testament is the history of salvation which centers around the history of Jesus.

DUNN, JAMES D. G. *Unity and Diversity in the New Testament: An Inquiry into the Character of Earliest Christianity.* Philadelphia: Westminster Press, 1977. A discussion of New Testament theology, first topically and then in terms of four types, with the assertion that the basic unity notwithstanding the diversity is constituted by an affirmation of the identity of Jesus and the risen Lord.

GÖPPELT, LEONHARD. *Theologie des Neuen Testament.* Edited by Jürgen Roloff. 2 vols. Göttingen: Vandenhoeck & Ruprecht, 1975–76. A posthumously published work in which Göppelt interprets the New Testament as the witness to an event which had its origin in the Old Testament and its fulfillment in Jesus. He did this in affirmation of the tradition of salvation history as it had been understood by Johann Christian Konrad von Hofmann (*Weissagung und Erfüllung im Alten und im Neuen Testament,* 1841–44) and by Adolf Schlatter.

JEREMIAS, JOACHIM. *Neutestamentliche Theologie, Erster Teil, Die Verkündigung Jesu.* Gütersloh: Gütersloher Verlagshaus Gerd Mohn, 1971. English translation, *New Testament Theology: The Preaching of Jesus.* Translated by John Bowden. New York: Charles Scribner's Sons / London: SCM Press, 1971. In this first volume, Jeremias relentlessly continues his quest to reconstruct the historical ministry of Jesus.

KÜMMEL, WERNER GEORG. *Die Theologie des Neuen Testaments nach seinen Hauptzeugen.* Göttingen: Vandenhoeck & Ruprecht, 1976. English translation, *The Theology of the New Testament According to its Main Witnesses—Jesus, Paul, John.* Translated by J. E. Steely. Nashville: Abingdon Press, 1973. Fundamental for Kümmel is the conception that the only access to an understanding of the New Testament writings is through historical inquiry, however, not in the sense of detachment but of intimate involvement which means, for him, to listen with ultimate openness.

MEINERTZ, MAX. *Theologie des Neuen Testaments.* 2 vols. Bonn: Peter Hanstein Verlag, 1950. Meinertz disclaims that this first comprehensive Roman Catholic New Testament theology is systematic. It presents the theological *substance (Gehalt)* of the New Testament in four main parts represented by Jesus, the primitive church, Paul, and John. The presentation is nevertheless not historical but the discussion of the theological substance in four historically distinct settings.

RICHARDSON, ALAN. *An Introduction to the Theology of the New Testament.* New York: Harper and Brothers, 1958. This is the clearest contemporary example of a New Testament theology that is based not on a critical investigation of the New Testament but on dogmatic presuppositions.

SCHELKLE, KARL HERRMANN. *Theologie des Neuen Testaments.* 4 vols. Düsseldorf: Patmos Verlag, 1968ff. English translation, *Theology of the New Testament.* Translated by William A. Jurgens. Collegeville, Minn.: Liturgical Press, 1971ff. A thoroughly systematic but not specifically dogmatic discussion under topical headings, but with individual New Testament writings under each heading, introduced by the Old Testament perspective.

SCOTT, ERNEST F. *The Varieties of New Testament Religion.* New York: Charles Scribner's Sons, 1943. This is one of the relatively few English language works which approaches the subject from the point of view of a history of religion.